# *Good For You Cakes!*

### Jane Marsh Dieckmann

The Crossing Press • Freedom • California 95019

*This book is dedicated to my loyal companions of the weekly stitch and support gatherings— Ellie, Gay, Nancy, and Wilda— all women with a concern for good health and nutritious eating, who have provided recipes, ideas, and love and who have consumed a great deal of cake.*

Cover illustration and design by Betsy Bayley
Medallions by Melanie Lofland Gendron

Printed in the U.S.A.

**Library of Congress Cataloging-in-Publication Data**
Dieckmann, Jane M.
    Good For You Cakes! / by Jane Marsh Dieckmann,
        p.  cm.
    Includes index.
    ISBN  0-89594-454-5 (paper) - - ISBN  0-89594-455-3 (cloth)
    1. Cake.   I. Title
TX771.D46  1991
641.8'653 - - dc20           91-6556
                    CIP

# Contents

# 1
# *About Cakes*

When I was growing up, we ate a lot more cake than we do today. It seemed the cakes were better, there was more time to make them, and not many people were concerned with diets and cholesterol counts. My family had cakes for everyone's birthday, of course, but we also produced them for any sort of party and as a frequent and routine dessert item. I can remember the children in the kitchen all trying to help make the cake and waiting for the bowl and beaters to lick. My favorite cake as a child (and even today) was a chocolate layer cake with fluffy frosting, and after we moved to the country (when I was seven), my mother's cook, who no longer worked for us, would make the trip every year on the bus to bake just such a cake for my birthday. So cakes have been special for me and, I would wager, for almost everyone, something very good to eat.

In today's world, cakes are popular still for birthday and wedding celebrations, for special parties, for the brunch and coffee break, the afternoon tea, and the after-school snack for children, and—often—when it is "time for a little something," as Winnie the Pooh would say. But, sad to tell, the homemade cake has fallen from favor. One reason is that many cooks perceive cakes as hard to make, as time consuming, as complicated. And that, even sadder to tell, has led to the enormous popularity of the cake mix. In my view, the cake mix turns out a mediocre product and, unless you doctor it considerably, there's none of the special excitement of a really good cake. And the various preservatives and other additives they contain give pause to many people. Unfortunately too, the homemade cake is seen to be sinfully rich and fattening, a kind of evil indulgence that will send our bodies down the road to bad health and certain overweight.

The main idea of this book is to present cakes that not only are appealing but will dispell some of the bad thoughts surrounding our favorite dessert. A cake does not have to be the least nutritional part of our meal, nor the least nutritional food we serve at parties, or teas, or brunches.

In fact, the cakes presented here are filled with good ingredients—the bounty of whole grains, the high protein and calcium content of lowfat yogurt and buttermilk, the vitamins and minerals and fiber of fruits and fruit juices, nuts, seeds—ingredients that make the calories count for something. And although this is not a diet book and we are not counting those calories one by one, the recipes here aim at lower fats and less sugar, and many will speak to cooks with special dietary concerns.

A variety of recipes are presented here, cakes for all possible uses—snacking cakes, dessert cakes, cakes for parties and celebrations, coffee and tea cakes, fruitcakes for holidays. And these cakes are not only nutritious but are, most important of all, delicious—with that special quality we associate with a special dessert. Most are easy to make, involving only a little more time than a mix. I am convinced, and I hope you will be too, that with a minimum of care and attention a scrumptious good-for-you cake is a fine and simple achievement.

## Ingredients

The principal ingredients required for baking a cake are easy to find. The basics are flours, shortening, sweeteners, eggs, liquids, and, of course, the various leavenings and flavorings such as baking powder, baking soda, salt, spices, and extracts. The extras are the fruits, nuts, seeds, nonfat dry milk powder, cheeses, and nutritional yeast.

*Flours, Grains, and Cereals.* By and large the flours used here can be interchangeable, but do

read the following carefully.

I use **all-purpose flour** for the white flour in my baking. Be sure that it is unbleached. I very rarely use white pastry flour, and the recipes here do not call for it. Because all-purpose flour is lighter in texture than the whole grain flours, it is an essential ingredient for most cakes. Also, whole grain flours are darker in color, and if you want to make a light-colored white cake, then some all-purpose flour is needed. It can be supplemented with soy flour, which is made from finely ground cooked and dried soybeans and which adds significant amounts of protein. Soy flour lacks gluten (leading to a heavy baked product) and has a very distinctive flavor (not popular to very many), and therefore cannot be used in large amounts. Do not substitute it for more than one-eighth of other flours. Another very useful "white" flour is oat flour, discussed below.

The whole grain flours contain the bran and the germ of the grain, which are a major source of B vitamins and vitamin E, as well as a good source of protein, calcium, and iron. Most of these elements have been processed out in the milling of all-purpose flour; some vitamins and minerals are put back into enriched white flour, but none of the natural fiber has been replaced. **Whole wheat pastry flour** works very well in cakes, especially the moist, dark ones, and clearly adds many important nutritional elements. **Wheat germ**, which will add protein, potassium, and phosphorus, B-1 and B-2 vitamins, and niacin to your cake, also is a beneficial ingredient; it adds a slight graininess to the texture, which in most cakes poses no problem at all. Be sure to keep wheat germ in the refrigerator, as it can become rancid. Although it is used much less frequently, **rye flour** is a good ingredient in cakes.

I have found that **oat flour** is an excellent ingredient in cake baking, as it creates a light and fine texture. Without attempting to enter into the oat bran controversy, I will say only that oats have the highest protein of the commonly eaten grains and are an excellent source of seven B vitamins, vitamin E, and nine different minerals.

You can make your own oat flour easily. Put rolled oats into your blender or food processor and whirl them until they become totally ground into flour; this takes 30 to 60 seconds. There will be a few flakes and some bran in the flour, which are important nutrients and cause no problem. To make 1 cup of oat flour, use 1 to 1 ½ cups rolled oats. Oat flour is a good ingredient for those "white" cakes as it is pale in color, and it has a marvelous taste. In your cakes you can substitute **up to but no more than** ⅓ of the white flour with oat flour. All these ingredients are readily available in bulk from a natural foods store and in packaged form at most supermarkets.

I do use some breakfast cereals in my cakes, principally rolled oats and granolas. In my experience, there is not much difference between regular and quick-cooking rolled oats. You should use quick-cooking oats where I have specified it, however. A staggering number of commercial cereals are available at the supermarkets. Do check the ingredient panels before you buy: look for whole grains, little salt, low or no sugar, and absolutely no additives. I find that Kellogg's® All-Bran cereal (which I recommend as it has less sugar than other brands) and Wheat Nutri-Grain® cereal (which has no sugar at all) go very well in cakes.

*Shortening.* And now for one of the ways to make a good cake even better for you: I have found that many cake recipes call for more shortening than is really needed. Therefore the recipes in this book have reduced amounts of fat in them. Butter, of course, provides an unmatched flavor in cakes, but very often the butter flavor does not predominate, and one can often substitute a shortening with less saturated fat and cholesterol. There is some butter in this book, but it is used only when needed.

For those concerned about cholesterol, there are recipes using oils (the best of these are the monounsaturated canola oil, and the polyunsaturated safflower, sunflower, and corn oil—in that and also provide the B vitamins, iron, and potassium, not to mention a pleasant, tasty crunch.

You can add dried fruits and nuts and seeds to all but the most delicate cakes. They will make a nutritious and welcome addition.

A list of ingredient substitutions and equivalents is given in the appendix.

## *Equipment*

Cake making is a great deal easier if you have an electric mixer, with two bowls (one for beating eggs and egg whites separately if necessary), and with various speeds. You will need some mixing bowls, a set of measuring spoons and cups, some solid wooden spoons, a flour sifter (I keep mine on a paper plate and sift the dry ingredients onto the plate, which can then be curled up slightly for easy emptying), and—that most marvelous of tools—the rubber scraper, which is the best for folding in ingredients and for getting every last bit of batter out of the bowl (no chance for bowl lickers in my kitchen!).

Baking pans in the correct sizes are important. Many recipes for sheet cakes and loaf cakes can be made in smaller sized pans. Just be sure you have approximately the same amount of surface and remember that a smaller cake will take less time to bake. You will need square pans, in both the traditional 8-inch and 9-inch sizes; rectangular pans (usually 8 inches by 11 inches, 9 inches by 13 inches, and 10 inches by 14 inches); loaf pans (usual size is 5 inches by 9 inches, with smaller loaf pans available as well); layer cake pans, in diameters of 8 and 9 inches; the tube or bundt pan, which comes 8, 9, and 10 inches in diameter and is about 6 inches deep; and muffin pans for cupcakes. A listing of various pan sizes and capacities is given in the appendix.

In most cases, the pan or pans should be well greased to facilitate the removal of the cake. Nonfat vegetable sprays are available for spraying the pans; my experience is that they work well for most cakes, but if the baking temperature is high, the spray burns. You can always use vegetable oil, as well as margarine, for greasing pans.

Although I am not strong on fancy equipment, I do find that a food processor and a blender are very useful aids, especially when you want to chop fruits and nuts, puree ingredients, or make your own oat flour. The Huguenot Torte in this book, a family favorite, used to require what seemed to be hours of chopping apples and nuts. With the food processor, all this is done in a minute or two, and the cake is in the oven that much sooner.

## Making Cakes

Chapter XXXI in the first version of Fannie Farmer's *The Boston Cooking-School Cook Book* (the first edition of which came out almost one hundred years ago) entitled "Cake" opens as follows: "The mixing and baking of cake requires more care and judgment than any other branch of cookery; notwithstanding, it seems the one most frequently attempted by the inexperienced." I wonder how the inexperienced got experience and, my, times have changed! Yes, you do have to measure carefully. Yes, you often have to treat the cake gently. Yes, you should take "care and judgment," but that is true of all cooking. But cake making is not difficult, and the cakes that require a truly delicate touch and a subtle culinary approach are few and far between.

Once you have your ingredients assembled and are ready to begin, the process is quick. I have a friend who whips up a basic cake in the time it takes to preheat the oven! I might add that Fannie Farmer goes on to say, "Look at the fire and replenish by sprinkling on a small quantity of coal if there is not sufficient heat to effect the baking." Indeed, times have changed, and if the general rules given here seem lengthy, I suggest you go back to early Fannie Farmer. Cake making today is a lark compared to those days.

The general procedure for making a cake is as follows:

(1) Have all ingredients at room temperature, which means taking the butter or

margarine, eggs, milk and/or fruit juice or fruit juice concentrate out of the refrigerator at least 30 minutes before you begin.

(2)  Preheat the oven to the desired temperature (the right temperature is important) and make sure the oven shelf is in the *center* of the oven.

(3)  Grease the cake pans needed and set aside.

(4)  Cream or blend the shortening with the sweetening, then add the eggs and beat until well blended.

(5)  Measure carefully; then sift or combine the dry ingredients and set aside.

(6)  Measure the liquid ingredients and set aside.

(7)  Mix the dry ingredients into the creamed mixture in the bowl, usually alternately with the liquid, *only until just blended.* Often this can—and should—be done by hand, and very lightly and quickly.

(8)  Add fruits or nuts or seeds, if called for.

(9)  Pour or spoon the cake batter into the prepared pans, filling only two-thirds full.

(10)  Bake for the required length of time. Check the cake for doneness by pressing gently on the top (the cake will be firm to the touch and should spring back) or by inserting a cake tester or broom straw or toothpick into the center of the cake (if it comes out clean, the cake is done). A cake that is ready to come out of the oven will pull away slightly from the sides of the pan.

(11)  Put the cake pan(s) on a metal rack or trivet to cool. As a general rule, cool for about 10 minutes, run a spatula around the edge of cake, and invert it onto the rack to finish cooling. Do not frost until the cake is cool, unless the recipe says to put something on top of a warm cake. Don't let the cake stay too long in the pan; you'll have trouble removing it.

## Storing Cakes

Almost all cakes will keep several days in a cool place, well covered. Most cakes can be frozen, and it is very handy to be able to cut off a slice for a snack. You need to wait only minutes before eating. Storing cake has never been much of a problem in my house. There usually isn't any left.

## About Yields

The size of the cake pan will tell you how big a cake is going to be. Determining a precise number of servings in a cake is really very difficult because so much depends on the type of cake (you can get many more pieces from a fine-grained pound cake or a compact fruitcake, for example, than from a tender or crumbly layer cake). Also, the size of the piece often depends on the appetite of the lucky person who will eat it. The yields are given here as guidelines only, so use your judgment. A safe rule is to bake a larger cake than you think you will need. You can always freeze the remainder.

# 2
# *Snacking Cakes*

The snacking cake, as its name implies, is eaten out of your hand and is easily portable—something for the picnic, the outdoor buffet, the afternoon treat. It usually is baked in a square or rectangular pan, is rather flat, and is unfrosted. The virtues of this cake are many—it is quickly made (and really doesn't require an electric mixer), is less delicate than other cakes and so is a great choice for Fannie Farmer's "inexperienced cook," is substantial enough to travel with ease, and serves as an excellent substitute for the ever-popular cookie because you can easily eat it with your fingers. And because the snacking cake is a simple, everyday, uncomplicated sort of cake, you don't need a special occasion to make one. This is great family food.

# Saucepan Fudge Cake

*This cake has a rich fudge taste and the concealed benefits of applesauce, fruit juice concentrate, bran cereal, and dry milk powder. I can guarantee that no one will know that it has any fruit in it at all.*

2 squares unsweetened baking chocolate
¼ cup vegetable oil
½ cup honey
¼ cup apple juice concentrate
2 eggs, slightly beaten
1 teaspoon vanilla extract
1 cup thick, slightly sweetened
    applesauce
½ cup Kellogg's All-Bran cereal
2 tablespoons nonfat dry milk powder
½ cup whole wheat pastry flour
1 teaspoon baking powder
½ teaspoon baking soda
¼ teaspoon salt
Powdered sugar (optional)

Preheat the oven to 350° F.

In a large saucepan, heat the chocolate and oil until the chocolate is melted. Then stir in the honey and juice concentrate. Add the beaten eggs, vanilla, and applesauce and stir well. Stir in the cereal and dry milk powder. Sift together the remaining ingredients, except the powdered sugar, and stir them in lightly, just enough to blend.

Bake in an ungreased 9-inch square pan 35 to 40 minutes. Cool. Dust with powdered sugar, if desired, and cut into squares.

Yield: 9 servings

# Carob Oatmeal Cake

*A dream treat for the person who can't eat chocolate, this cake goes marvelously with hot Cherry Sauce (page 141). And with rolled oats, cottage cheese, yogurt, and nuts, it is an excellent source of protein.*

¼ cup vegetable oil
¼ cup honey
¼ cup plain lowfat yogurt
1 cup cottage cheese
2 eggs
1 teaspoon almond extract
1 cup whole wheat pastry flour
¼ cup all-purpose flour
½ cup carob powder or ⅓ cup cocoa
1 teaspoon baking powder
1 teaspoon baking soda
¼ teaspoon salt
1 cup rolled oats
½ cup chopped walnuts or almonds

Preheat the oven to 350° F. Grease a 9-inch by 13-inch rectangular pan.

Blend the oil, honey, and yogurt, beating well. Beat in the cottage cheese; then add the eggs, one at a time, beating well. Stir in the almond extract.

Combine the flours, carob, baking powder, baking soda, salt, and oats. Gradually add them to the liquid mixture, blending well. Stir in the nuts.

Pour the batter into the prepared pan, and bake for 30 to 35 minutes. Cool and cut into squares.

Yield: 12 to 15 servings

# Yogurt Poppy Seed Cake

*Another traditional snacking cake, this one is moist and provides the extra protein of yogurt and oat flour.*

1 cup plain lowfat yogurt
½ cup sugar
2 tablespoons melted butter
2 tablespoons vegetable oil
2 eggs
1 teaspoon vanilla extract
1 cup all-purpose flour
1 teaspoon baking soda
¼ teaspoon salt
½ cup oat flour
⅓ cup poppy seeds
Powdered sugar (optional)

Preheat the oven to 350° F. Grease a 9-inch springform or an 8-inch square baking pan.

In a large bowl, stir together the yogurt, sugar, and liquid shortening until well blended. With a wooden spoon, beat in the eggs until the mixture is smooth, then stir in the vanilla.

Sift together the flour, baking soda, and salt. Mix in the oat flour. Add the flour mixture and the poppy seeds to the wet ingredients all at once. Stir until smooth.

Pour into the prepared pan, and bake for 50 minutes, or until the top is brown and firm to the touch. If desired, dust the top of the cooled cake with powdered sugar.

Yield: 6 to 9 servings

## Variations

**Orange Syrup Yogurt Cake.** Omit the poppy seeds and substitute 1 teaspoon lemon extract for the vanilla extract. While the cake is baking, prepare the syrup by combining ½ cup orange juice concentrate, ½ cup water, 2 tablespoons honey, and 1 tablespoon grated orange rind. Bring to a boil, stirring constantly, and boil 3 minutes. Cool and stir in 2 tablespoons Cointreau or Grand Marnier (if desired). Pierce the warm cake deeply with a cake tester or fork and pour the warm syrup evenly over the top. Let stand for 30 minutes before slicing.

**Honey Yogurt Cake.** Omit the poppy seeds. Substitute ¼ cup dark honey for the sugar and sift 1 teaspoon each of cinnamon and ginger in with the dry ingredients. Bake for 45 to 50 minutes.

**Yogurt Raisin Loaf.** Omit the poppy seeds and add ½ cup raisins, which you have lightly floured, to the batter. Bake in a greased 5-inch by 9-inch loaf pan at 375° F. for 45 minutes.

**Lemon Yogurt Cake.** Omit the poppy seeds and stir in 2 tablespoons grated lemon rind and the juice of ½ lemon. Bake in a greased 5-inch by 9-inch loaf pan at 375° F. for about 45 minutes.

# *Oatmeal Honey Nut Cake*

❖❖❖❖❖❖❖❖❖❖❖❖❖❖❖❖❖❖❖❖❖❖❖❖❖❖❖❖❖❖❖❖❖❖❖

½ cup water
¼ cup honey
¼ cup apple or grape juice concentrate
1 cup quick-cooking rolled oats
2 eggs
2 tablespoons brown sugar
¼ cup vegetable oil
1 teaspoon grated lemon rind
1 cup whole wheat pastry flour
1 teaspoon baking soda
1 teaspoon cinnamon
¼ teaspoon salt
1 cup chopped walnuts
Powdered sugar (optional)

Preheat the oven to 350° F. Grease a 9-inch square pan.

Combine the water, honey, and juice concentrate in a saucepan and heat to boiling. Stir in the oats and let stand for 20 minutes.

Beat the eggs and brown sugar together until well blended. Beat in the oil and rind.

Sift together the flour, baking soda, cinnamon, and salt. Add to the liquid mixture along with the oatmeal; blend well. Stir in the walnuts.

Bake for 45 minutes. Cool. Dust with powdered sugar.

Yield: 9 servings

# Carrot Applesauce Cake

½ cup firmly packed light brown sugar
1 cup thick, slightly sweetened
    applesauce
⅓ cup vegetable oil
2 eggs
1 cup whole wheat pastry flour
½ cup all-purpose flour
1 teaspoon cinnamon
1 teaspoon baking powder
½ teaspoon baking soda
½ teaspoon salt
1 cup rolled oats
⅓ cup wheat germ
1 cup shredded carrots, firmly packed
Creamy Cheese Topping (page 136)
    (optional)

Preheat the oven to 350° F. Grease a 9-inch square pan well.

Combine the brown sugar, applesauce, and oil in a large mixing bowl; add the eggs, one at a time, beating well after each addition.

Sift together the flours, cinnamon, baking powder, baking soda, and salt. Stir in the oats and wheat germ and mix well until blended. Then stir in the carrots.

Spread the batter in the prepared pan, and bake for 35 to 40 minutes, or until the cake tests done. It can be served plain, but for a traditional carrot cake, spread the cooled cake with the Creamy Cheese topping.

Yield: 9 servings

# Amazing Raisin Spice Cake

*For anyone watching cholesterol and satu-
rated fats, here is the cake to choose because
it contains no eggs and no solid shortening.
Also notable is its whole grain and fruit
content. The entire cake is mixed in one
saucepan.*

¹/₂ cup apple juice concentrate
2 cups raisins
¹/₂ cup water
¹/₄ cup dark honey
2 tablespoons dark brown sugar
¹/₃ cup vegetable oil
¹/₂ teaspoon cinnamon
¹/₂ teaspoon allspice
¹/₄ teaspoon nutmeg
¹/₄ teaspoon salt
¹/₂ cup all-purpose flour

¹/₂ cup whole wheat pastry flour
1 teaspoon baking powder
1 teaspoon baking soda
¹/₂ cup oat flour
¹/₃ cup wheat germ
1 cup chopped nuts (optional)
Powdered sugar or Easy Glaze
    (page 138) (optional)

In a large saucepan, combine the juice concentrate, raisins, water, honey, brown sugar,
oil, spices, and salt. Bring to a boil, reduce
the heat, and simmer for 3 minutes. Set aside
to cool.

Preheat the oven to 350° F. Grease a 9-
inch tube pan very well, using vegetable oil.

Sift together the all-purpose and whole
wheat flours, baking powder, and baking

soda; stir in the oat flour and wheat germ. Slowly mix these dry ingredients into the cooled liquid and beat the batter until it is smooth. Add 1 cup chopped nuts, if desired.

Pour the batter into the prepared pan, and bake for about 1 hour. Cool the cake. Serve plain, dusted with powdered sugar, or with the glaze poured over.

Yield: 6 to 8 servings

## *Variation*

**Amazing Apricot Spice Cake.** Substitute 1 cup chopped apricots for the 1 cup raisins and increase the brown sugar to ¼ cup.

# Apple Raisin Cake

This traditional cake is filled with apples, raisins, and nuts. It has been, and probably always will be, one of the most popular afternoon treats for children coming home from school.

**1 cup whole wheat pastry flour**
**½ cup all-purpose flour**
**½ cup rye flour**
**2 teaspoons baking soda**
**2 teaspoons cinnamon**
**¼ teaspoon nutmeg**
**¼ teaspoon salt**
**2 eggs**
**½ cup honey**
**2 tablespoons butter, softened**
**2 tablespoons margarine, softened**
**2 teaspoons vanilla extract**

**4 cups chopped or coarsely grated apples (do not peel)**
**1 cup raisins or chopped dates**
**1 cup chopped walnuts**

Preheat the oven to 350° F.

Sift together the flours, baking soda, spices, and salt; set aside.

In a large mixing bowl, beat together the eggs, honey, butter, margarine, and vanilla until smooth and fluffy. Stir in the dry ingredients. Lightly fold in the apples and raisins.

Spread the batter in an ungreased 9-inch by 13-inch baking pan and sprinkle the nuts on top. Bake for 35 to 40 minutes. Cool and cut into bars or squares.

Yield: 12 to 15 servings

# Gingerbread

◆◇◆◇◆◇◆◇◆◇◆◇◆◇◆◇◆◇◆◇◆◇◆◇◆◇◆◇◆◇◆◇◆◇◆◇◆◇◆

1 cup whole wheat pastry flour
½ cup rye flour
½ cup all-purpose flour
½ cup wheat germ
2 tablespoons sugar
2 tablespoons nonfat dry milk powder
1 teaspoon baking soda
¼ teaspoon salt
1½ teaspoons ginger
1 teaspoon cinnamon
¼ teaspoon cloves
2 eggs, well beaten
¾ cup buttermilk
½ cup apple juice concentrate
½ cup dark molasses
¼ cup vegetable oil
Hot Applesauce Topping (page 145)

Preheat the oven to 350° F. Grease a 9-inch square baking pan.

Combine the dry ingredients in a bowl and stir well. Blend the beaten eggs with the other liquid ingredients and pour them over the dry ingredients. Mix thoroughly.

Pour the batter into the prepared pan, and bake for 35 to 40 minutes. Cool for about 10 minutes before removing from the pan. Cut into squares. Serve warm just plain or covered with the topping or with Lemon Sauce (page 146).

Yield: 9 servings

# *Carrot Raisin Cake*

Here is another amazing cake—moist, dark, spicy, and without eggs. You can substitute 1 tablespoon oil for the butter and you will have another delicious choice for those watching their cholesterol and saturated fat intake. In addition, this cake brings the boost of vitamin A from the carrots; high fiber, calcium, potassium, and iron from the raisins; protein from the nuts; plus the benefits of whole grains.

This cake needs to be started some time before you eat it, so be sure to schedule accordingly.

¼ cup dark honey
¼ cup apple juice concentrate
1⅓ cups water
1 cup raisins
1 tablespoon butter or vegetable oil
2 large carrots, finely grated
1 teaspoon cinnamon
½ teaspoon cloves
½ teaspoon nutmeg
1 cup chopped walnuts
1 cup whole wheat pastry flour
½ cup all-purpose flour
½ cup wheat germ
½ cup oat bran
2 teaspoons baking powder
1 teaspoon baking soda
½ teaspoon salt

Combine the honey, juice concentrate, water, raisins, butter, carrots, and spices in a large saucepan. Bring to a boil and simmer for 5 minutes. Cover the pan and let the mixture rest for 12 hours to blend the flavors well. If the weather is very warm, put the mixture to rest in a cool place.

Preheat the oven to 275° F. Grease a 10-inch tube pan or two 5-inch by 9-inch loaf pans well.

Combine the remaining dry ingredients, mixing together thoroughly. Stir them into the liquid and blend everything.

Pour into the prepared pan(s), and bake for 2 hours. Cool, then wrap in foil. This cake keeps well and freezes well.

Yield: 9 to 12 servings

## *Variation*

**Orange-Date Carrot Cake.** In place of the honey and apple juice concentrate, use ½ cup orange juice concentrate. Substitute 1 cup chopped dates for the raisins.

# Zucchini Cake

1 tablespoon active dry yeast
½ cup sweet cider, lukewarm
2 cups finely grated zucchini,
   packed well
¼ cup light molasses
¼ cup vegetable oil
1 large egg, well beaten
⅓ cup buttermilk
1 cup cornmeal
1 cup whole wheat flour
1 teaspoon cinnamon
½ teaspoon nutmeg
½ teaspoon allspice
½ teaspoon cloves
2 tablespoons nutritional yeast
1 tablespoon nonfat dry milk powder
½ cup raisins
½ cup chopped walnuts (optional)
Creamy Cheese Topping (page 136)

Grease an 8-inch by 12-inch (or 9-inch by 11-inch) pan. Dissolve the yeast in the warm cider. Set aside. Blend the zucchini, molasses, oil, egg, and buttermilk in a large mixing bowl. Stir in the dissolved yeast. Then stir in the remaining ingredients. Pour into prepared pan. Let the cake rest in a warm place for 20 to 30 minutes to rise slightly.

Preheat the oven to 350° F. while the cake is rising.

Gently place the cake in the preheated oven and bake for 40 minutes. Cool, then serve plain or frost with the topping.

Yield: 12 servings

# Pumpkin Cake

1½ cups whole wheat pastry flour
¼ cup all-purpose flour
¼ cup oat flour
1 tablespoon baking powder
1 teaspoon baking soda
¼ teaspoon salt
1 tablespoon cinnamon
½ teaspoon cloves
½ teaspoon nutmeg
¼ teaspoon ginger
⅓ cup vegetable oil
¼ cup buttermilk or skim milk
⅓ cup pitted dates, well packed
¾ cup canned or fresh pumpkin puree
¾ cup slightly sweetened applesauce
1 large egg
½ cup roasted soy grits or chopped
   walnuts
1 cup raisins

Preheat the oven to 350° F. Grease a 9-inch by 13-inch pan.

In a large mixing bowl, combine the flours, baking powder, baking soda, salt, and spices.

In a food processor or blender, process the oil, buttermilk, dates, pumpkin, applesauce, and egg. Continue processing until the dates are chopped finely and the mixture is smooth.

Pour the blended mixture into the dry ingredients. Mix until smooth, then stir in the soy grits and raisins. Spread in the prepared pan, smoothing evenly to the edges. Bake for 40 minutes. Cool and cut into squares.

Yield: 12 to 15 servings

# Fresh Rhubarb Cake

³/₄ cup light honey
¹/₄ cup apple juice concentrate
¹/₃ cup vegetable oil
2 large eggs
³/₄ cup buttermilk
2 cups whole wheat pastry flour
1 teaspoon baking soda
¹/₄ teaspoon salt
2 cups finely cut fresh rhubarb
¹/₄ cup wheat germ
¹/₄ cup oat bran

**Topping**
¹/₄ cup brown or white sugar
¹/₂ teaspoon cinnamon
¹/₄ cup finely chopped walnuts

Preheat the oven to 350° F. Grease well one 9-inch by 13-inch pan or two 8-inch square pans.

In a large bowl, mix together the honey, juice concentrate, oil, eggs, and buttermilk and beat very well. Then stir in the flour, baking soda, and salt. Mix the rhubarb with the wheat germ and oat bran and stir it in.

Pour the batter into the prepared pan. Combine the topping ingredients and sprinkle over the top of the batter.

Bake for 40 minutes or until the cake starts pulling away from the edge of the pan.

Yield: 12 to 16 servings

# *Applesauce Banana Cake*

1 cup all-purpose flour
1 cup whole wheat pastry flour
¼ cup soy flour
1 tablespoon nutritional yeast
1 teaspoon baking powder
1 teaspoon baking soda
1 teaspoon cinnamon
½ teaspoon cloves
½ teaspoon allspice
½ teaspoon salt
¼ cup wheat germ
½ cup honey
½ cup apple juice concentrate
¼ cup plain lowfat yogurt
¼ cup vegetable oil
2 tablespoons margarine, very soft
1 cup slightly sweetened applesauce
1 cup mashed ripe bananas
2 eggs

½ cup chopped peanuts or walnuts
¾ cup raisins
Powdered sugar

Preheat the oven to 350° F. Grease a 9-inch by 13-inch pan.

Into the large bowl of the electric mixer, sift all the dry ingredients, except the wheat germ; stir in the wheat germ. Add the honey, juice concentrate, yogurt, oil, margarine, applesauce, and bananas. Blend well, then beat at medium speed until creamy. Add the eggs and beat for 2 minutes at medium speed. Stir in the nuts and raisins.

Bake for about 45 minutes. Turn out onto a cake rack, and while still warm, sift powdered sugar lightly over the top.

Yield: 16 servings

27

# Apple Betty Crunch Cake

This cake has a flavor and consistency reminiscent of an old-fashioned apple brown betty, but with no butter and a lot less sugar. Part of the crunch comes from the cereal.

**Topping**
1/3 cup Kellogg's 40% Bran Flakes
1/4 cup brown sugar
1/4 teaspoon cinnamon
2 tablespoons margarine

**Cake**
1/2 cup all-purpose flour
1/2 cup whole wheat pastry flour
1/4 cup wheat germ
2 tablespoons dry milk powder
2 teaspoons baking powder
1/4 teaspoon salt

1 cup Kellogg's 40% Bran Flakes,
  crushed to measure 1/2 cup
1/2 cup apple juice concentrate
1 teaspoon grated lemon rind
3 tablespoons margarine or vegetable oil
1/4 cup light brown sugar
1 egg
1 1/2 cups finely chopped apples
1/2 cup raisins

Mix together the topping ingredients, until crumbly. Set aside.

Preheat the oven to 350° F. Grease a 9-inch square pan.

Stir together the flours, wheat germ, dry milk powder, baking powder, salt, and crushed cereal. Set aside. Combine the juice concentrate and lemon rind and set aside.

In a large mixing bowl, beat together the margarine, brown sugar, and egg until smooth. Add the flour mixture alternately with the juice concentrate and lemon rind, mixing well with each addition. Stir in the apples and raisins.

Spread the batter in the prepared pan and sprinkle the topping evenly over the top. Bake for about 35 minutes, or until a tester inserted into the cake comes out clean. This is wonderful with vanilla ice cream, Custard Sauce (page 149), or Light Whipped Topping (page 138).

Yield: 9 to 12 servings

### *Variation*
**Nutri-Grain Apple Crunch Cake.** Substitute Kellogg's Nutri-Grain with Almonds for the 40% Bran Flakes in both the topping and the cake, making everything even crunchier.

# *Orange Raisin Cake*

❖➤❖➤❖➤❖➤❖➤❖➤❖➤❖➤❖➤❖➤❖➤❖➤❖➤❖➤❖➤❖➤❖➤❖➤❖➤❖➤❖➤❖➤❖➤❖➤❖

1 orange (select a juicy variety)
1 cup raisins
¹/₃ cup light honey
¹/₄ cup light brown sugar
2 tablespoons vegetable oil
2 tablespoons margarine
1 egg
1 cup buttermilk or sour skim milk
1 cup whole wheat pastry flour
¹/₂ cup all-purpose flour
1 teaspoon baking soda
¹/₄ teaspoon salt
¹/₂ cup wheat germ
¹/₂ cup powdered sugar

Remove the seeds and some pith from the orange. Grind it with the raisins in a meat grinder. Reserve 2 tablespoons of this mixture for the glaze.

Preheat the oven to 350° F. Grease a 7-inch by 11-inch pan or 9-inch square baking pan. Blend the honey, brown sugar, oil, and margarine in a mixing bowl; add the egg and beat thoroughly. Then add the buttermilk and mix well. Sift together the flours, baking soda, and salt; stir in the wheat germ. Mix the dry ingredients into the wet. Blend in the orange-raisin mixture (except what you have reserved).

Spread the batter in the pan and bake for 40 minutes. While the cake is still hot, spread it with a glaze made from the reserved orange-raisin mixture, the powdered sugar, and enough water or orange juice to make a medium-thin glaze.

This cake keeps well and freezes well.

Yield: 9 servings

# Cranberry and Honey Cake

*Cranberries provide important amounts of vitamin C. They have a short season, coming on the market for the Thanksgiving holiday and disappearing soon after. Fortunately they can be frozen for use all year-round. Be sure to defrost them before using for baking.*

1 large egg
¾ cup light honey
¼ cup apple juice concentrate
¼ cup plain lowfat yogurt
2 cups raw cranberries
1½ cups whole wheat pastry flour
½ cup wheat germ
1 teaspoon baking soda
½ teaspoon salt
1 cup sunflower seeds, chopped
2 tablespoons grated orange rind

Preheat the oven to 350° F. Grease a 10-inch tube pan well.

Combine the egg, honey, juice concentrate, yogurt, and cranberries in a food processor or blender. Process at low speed, pulsing off and on, until the berries are in small chunks. Scrape into a large mixing bowl.

Stir in the flour and wheat germ, then the baking soda and salt and mix very well. Add the seeds and orange rind and stir until well mixed.

Pour into the prepared pan, and bake for 45 to 50 minutes, or until a tester inserted into the cake comes out clean. Cool well before serving.

Yield: 12 servings

# Lemon Cake

⟡⟡⟡⟡⟡⟡⟡⟡⟡⟡⟡⟡⟡⟡⟡⟡⟡⟡⟡⟡⟡⟡⟡⟡⟡⟡⟡⟡⟡⟡⟡⟡⟡⟡⟡⟡⟡

⅓ cup vegetable oil
½ cup honey
⅔ cup plain lowfat yogurt
2 tablespoons lemon rind
2 tablespoons lemon juice
½ teaspoon vanilla extract
¼ cup nonfat dry milk powder
1½ cups whole wheat pastry flour
½ cup quick cooking rolled oats
2 tablespoons wheat germ
1 teaspoon baking powder
1 teaspoon baking soda
½ cup poppy seeds or finely chopped
   walnuts   (optional)
Lemon Yogurt Glaze (page 139)

Preheat the oven to 350° F. Grease well a 9-inch round layer pan or 8-inch square pan.

Combine the oil, honey, and yogurt in a large mixing bowl and whisk well. Stir in the lemon rind, lemon juice, vanilla, and dry milk powder; blend well.

Combine the flour, rolled oats, and wheat germ in a bowl; add the baking powder and baking soda and mix. Blend in the liquid ingredients quickly and thoroughly. If desired, you can add the poppy seeds or chopped walnuts.

Pour the batter into the prepared pan, and bake for 30 minutes. If a moister and more lemony cake is desired, cover the warm cake with Lemon Yogurt Glaze.

Yield: 9 servings

# 3
# *Cupcakes*

Cupcakes are really an extension of snacking cakes, having an uncomplicated portability as their main virtue. Many mothers have solved the gooey frosted birthday cake problem with a cupcake for each small guest, not a bad solution. Although many cake batters make good cupcakes, the following are particularly good for this special kind of small cake, with unusual and fun ingredients.

Cupcakes are most easily baked in muffin tins, if you have them. Pyrex custard cups are all right, but you should decrease the oven temperature by 25 degrees. Make sure that whatever you use is well greased. Paper liners are a great help in the cleanup, although I have always been bothered by all that wasted cake sticking to the paper. And so, if you want to scrape your paper liner with a knife or even lick it, I'll always look the other way. Do avoid the fancy foil colored liners. We really don't know how much of the foil or the color might end up in our insides or what they might do there.

# *One-Egg Cupcakes*

*Here is a basic plain recipe for cupcakes. Feel free to add any of the following to the recipe for variation: 2 tablespoons poppy seeds; ¹/₂ cup chopped nuts, ¹/₂ cup dried fruit—raisins, dates, currants, or apricots. Or try a different flavor of fruit juice concentrate or add ¹/₂ cup chocolate chips.*

*These cupcakes are rather light and tender, so do use paper liners in the muffin cups.*

¹/₄ cup vegetable oil
1 teaspoon vanilla extract
¹/₂ cup light honey
¹/₄ cup apple juice concentrate
1 large egg
¹/₂ cup plain lowfat yogurt
1¹/₂ cups whole wheat pastry flour
1 teaspoon baking soda
¹/₄ teaspoon salt
Milk and Honey Glaze (page 139)
   (optional)

Preheat the oven to 350° F. Line 16 muffin cups with paper liners.

Mix together the oil, vanilla, honey, juice concentrate, egg, and yogurt in a large bowl, beating until well blended.

Sift together the flour, baking soda, and salt. Stir into the liquid mixture. Divide the batter evenly among the lined muffin cups. Bake for 20 to 25 minutes, or until the tops are golden brown. Cool and serve plain or topped with the glaze.

Yield: 16 cupcakes

# Applesauce Spice Cupcakes

*Here is a tasty combination with applesauce, spices, and rolled oats.*

**3 tablespoons butter, softened**
**2 tablespoons margarine, softened**
**¼ cup apple juice concentrate**
**1 egg**
**¾ cup slightly sweetened applesauce**
**1 cup all-purpose flour**
**½ cup whole wheat pastry flour**
**1 teaspoon baking soda**
**1 teaspoon cinnamon**
**¼ teaspoon nutmeg**
**¼ teaspoon salt**
**1 cup rolled oats**
**½ cup buttermilk or plain lowfat yogurt**
**Milk and Honey Glaze or Lemon Yogurt**
**    Glaze (page 139)**

Preheat the oven to 375° F. Grease 12 muffin cups.

In a large mixing bowl, blend the butter, margarine, juice concentrate, and egg. Beat well, then stir in the applesauce.

Sift together the flours, baking soda, spices, and salt; mix in the rolled oats. Add the dry ingredients to the liquid mixture alternately with the buttermilk, beginning and ending with dry ingredients.

Pour the batter into the muffin cups, filling about ¾ full. Bake for 20 to 25 minutes. Cool. Spread the tops with the glaze.

Yield: 12 cupcakes

# *Molasses Cupcakes*

*These cupcakes have the natural flavoring of sweet cider and molasses, with a nutritional boost from whole wheat flour, dry milk powder, and nutritional yeast. Because they are made with baker's yeast, be sure to allow time for them to rise.*

**1 tablespoon active dry yeast**
**1 cup sweet cider, warmed**
**½ cup light molasses**
**1½ cups whole wheat pastry flour**
**½ cup wheat germ**
**1 tablespoon nutritional yeast**
**⅓ cup vegetable oil**
**1 tablespoon grated lemon rind**
**1 egg, well beaten**

Soften the dry yeast in the warm cider. Measure the molasses and add 1 tablespoon of it along with 1 cup of the flour to the yeast mixture. Mix well. Let the sponge stand until bubbly. Then add the remaining molasses, flour, and all the other ingredients. Beat the batter thoroughly.

Put the batter into 12 well-oiled muffin tins, filling halfway. Let rise in a warm place until doubled in bulk, 45 to 60 minutes.

When the cupcakes have almost finished rising, preheat the oven to 350° F. Bake the cakes for about 20 minutes, or until a tester inserted into a cupcake comes out clean. Cool.

Yield: 12 cupcakes

# Easy Date-Nut Cupcakes

1 cup chopped dates
½ cup water
½ cup orange juice concentrate
1 teaspoon baking soda
2 teaspoons grated orange rind
1 egg, well beaten
1 tablespoon dark brown sugar
1 tablespoon margarine
2 tablespoons nonfat dry milk powder
1 cup whole wheat pastry flour
½ cup wheat germ
¼ teaspoon salt
½ cup chopped walnuts
Milk and Honey Glaze (page 139) or
   Creamy Cheese Topping (page 136)
   (optional)

Measure the dates and put in a bowl. Heat the water and juice concentrate to boiling and pour over the dates. Stir in the baking soda and orange rind and allow to cool.

Preheat the oven to 400° F. Line 12 muffin cups with paper liners.

In a large bowl, mix together the egg, brown sugar, margarine, and dry milk until well blended. Stir in the cooled date mixture. Then add the flour, wheat germ, and salt, along with the chopped nuts.

Pour into the muffin tins and bake for 20 minutes. Cool and serve plain or frosted.

Yield: 12 cupcakes

# Cocoa-Banana Cupcakes

*These cupcakes are light and tender, with that wonderful flavor combination of bananas and chocolate.*

1 cup all-purpose flour
¼ cup whole wheat pastry flour
¼ cup oat flour
2 tablespoons cocoa or carob powder
1½ teaspoons baking powder
1 tablespoon nutritional yeast
1 tablespoon nonfat dry milk powder
¼ cup margarine, softened
¼ cup light honey
1 egg
1 cup mashed ripe bananas
⅔ cup skim or 2% lowfat milk
½ teaspoon vanilla extract

Preheat the oven to 350° F. Line 12 muffin cups with paper liners.

Combine the flours, cocoa, baking powder, yeast, and dry milk powder in a small bowl, stirring well.

Cream the margarine, gradually adding in the honey, egg, and bananas; beat well. Then add the dry ingredients alternately with the milk and vanilla. Begin and end with dry ingredients.

Spoon into the muffin cups. Bake for 25 to 30 minutes. Cool.

Yield: 12 cupcakes

# 4
# *Dessert Cakes*

Here are the more delicate cakes, the fancier cakes, cakes with frostings, fruit, and sauces. You need a fork to eat them and you probably should eat them sitting down.

The frosted layer cake represents the true birthday and celebration cake for most of us. When you make one, be sure to measure very accurately and follow directions very carefully. The sponge cakes and angel food cakes use many eggs, which gives them a light and springy texture. Generally they contain no shortening and are usually baked in a tube pan. The chiffon cakes, developed some years ago by General Mills, are made with oil and are very light in texture. For these cakes, be sure the eggs are at room temperature (take them out about 1 hour in advance) and be sure too to treat the batter gently and lightly. Cut these cakes with a serrated knife, sawing back and forth. They can be served plain, but are really best with a topping of fruit, sauce, whipped cream, ice cream, or custard.

The torte is a fancy dessert cake of European origin. Like a sponge cake, it depends on many eggs but differs in that it is a flat cake, usually made with finely chopped or ground nuts, with only small amounts of flour. Traditionally, tortes are served with piles of stiffly whipped cream. The tortes here can be served just plain or with the much healthier Light Whipped Topping (page 138). And, finally, we have the upside-down cakes, the pudding cakes, and the cakes with sauces. These are the cakes that you must often eat with a spoon. Here too are the shortcakes (less short than you'll find elsewhere) and the old-fashioned dessert cakes that somehow spell down-home cooking and family food. As for many frostings and glazes that go with dessert cakes, I have cut down on sweetening and eliminated buttercream frostings altogether.

# Plain and Simple Cocoa Cake

2 tablespoons butter or margarine
¾ cup sugar
3 tablespoons unsweetened baking cocoa
1 egg
1½ cups all-purpose flour
½ cup whole wheat pastry flour
1 teaspoon baking powder
⅛ teaspoon salt
1 cup buttermilk or sour skim milk
1 teaspoon baking soda
Fluffy Frosting (page 135), Creamy
   Cheese Topping (page 136), or
   Lemon Yogurt Glaze (page 139)

Preheat the oven to 350° F. Grease a 9-inch square pan.

Cream the butter with the sugar; blend in the cocoa. Beat in the egg.

Sift together the flours, baking powder, and salt. Combine the buttermilk and baking soda. Gently add the dry ingredients to the creamed mixture alternately with the buttermilk.

Pour the batter into the prepared pan and bake for 30 minutes. Cool and then frost.

Yield: 9 servings

# Super Chocolate Cake

¼ cup vegetable oil
2 tablespoons margarine
½ cup honey
1 teaspoon vanilla extract
2 eggs
1 cup whole wheat pastry flour
¼ cup oat flour
½ cup rolled oats
1 teaspoon baking powder
1 teaspoon baking soda
¼ teaspoon salt
⅓ cup unsweetened baking cocoa
⅓ cup orange juice concentrate
½ cup buttermilk or plain lowfat yogurt
Fluffy Frosting (page 135)

Preheat the oven to 350° F. Grease and flour two 8-inch layer pans.

Cream together the oil, margarine, and honey until well blended. Beat in the vanilla and eggs; continue beating until light.

Combine the flours, rolled oats (which you can whirl briefly in the food processor to cut up somewhat), baking powder, baking soda, salt, and cocoa.

Combine the juice concentrate and buttermilk. Add the dry ingredients to the creamed mixture alternately with the wet, in 3 portions, starting and ending with the dry ingredients.

Pour the batter into the prepared pans, and bake the layers for 30 minutes. Cool and frost.

Yield: 12 servings

# Lemon Layer Cake

1¼ cups sifted all-purpose flour
2 tablespoons soy flour
1½ teaspoons baking powder
1 teaspoon baking soda
¼ teaspoon salt
¼ cup oat flour
2 tablespoons nonfat dry milk powder
¼ cup buttermilk
¼ cup white grape juice concentrate
¼ cup fresh lemon juice
1 tablespoon grated lemon rind
¼ cup butter
½ cup sugar
3 eggs
Lemon Cake Filling (page 148)
Light Butter Frosting (page 134)

Preheat the oven to 350° F. Grease and flour two 8-inch layer pans.

Sift together the flours, baking powder, baking soda, and salt. Stir in the oat flour and dry milk powder and set aside.

In a measuring cup, combine the buttermilk, concentrate, and lemon juice and rind.

In a large mixing bowl, cream the butter until light and add the sugar slowly, beating well. Add the eggs, one at a time, and beat well after each addition. Add the dry ingredients alternately with the buttermilk mixture, in 3 parts, blending well after each addition.

Divide the batter evenly between the pans, and bake for 25 minutes. Cool, remove from the pans, and spread the filling on the flat side of one layer. Place the second layer, flat side down, on top. Frost over the top and sides.

Yield: 12 servings

# *Orange Raisin Nut Cake*

◆▸◆▸◆▸◆▸◆▸◆▸◆▸◆▸◆▸◆▸◆▸◆▸◆▸◆▸◆▸◆▸◆▸◆▸◆▸◆▸◆▸◆▸◆▸◆▸◆▸◆▸◆▸◆▸◆▸◆▸◆▸

1 cup all-purpose flour
½ cup oat flour
2 tablespoons soy flour
2 tablespoons nonfat dry milk powder
½ cup sugar
½ teaspoon salt
½ cup orange juice concentrate
¾ cup buttermilk
¼ cup butter, softened
2 large eggs
1 teaspoon vanilla extract
¾ cup golden raisins, finely chopped
½ cup finely chopped walnuts or almonds
1 tablespoon grated orange rind
Creamy Filling (page 148)
Orange Fluffy Frosting (page 135)

Preheat the oven to 350° F. Grease and flour two 8-inch layer pans.

Measure the dry ingredients into a large mixing bowl and stir. Add the remaining ingredientw and blend for ½ minute on low speed, scraping the bowl constantly. Beat for 3 minutes on high speed, scraping occasionally.

Pour into the prepared pans, and bake 35 minutes. Cool and spread layer with the filling. Cover the top with the frosting, to which you have added 1 tablespoon orange rind.

Yield: 12 servings

# Applesauce-Oatmeal Cake

**◆▸◆▸◆▸◆▸◆▸◆▸◆▸◆▸◆▸◆▸◆▸◆▸◆▸◆▸◆▸◆▸◆▸◆▸◆▸◆▸◆▸◆▸**

1 cup whole wheat pastry flour
¼ cup soy flour
¼ cup all-purpose flour
1 teaspoon baking powder
½ teaspoon baking soda
¼ teaspoon salt
1 teaspoon cinnamon
½ teaspoon nutmeg
¼ teaspoon cloves
½ cup rolled oats or crushed bran flakes
¾ cup raisins
2 tablespoons butter
2 tablespoons margarine
¼ cup honey
1 large egg
1 cup slightly sweetened applesauce
½ cup apple juice concentrate

1 teaspoon grated lemon rind
1 teaspoon vanilla extract
**Light Butter Frosting (page 134)**
½ cup finely chopped walnuts (optional)

Preheat the oven to 375° F. Grease and flour a 9-inch square baking pan. Sift together the flours, baking powder, baking soda, salt, and spices; stir in the rolled oats and raisins.

In a large mixing bowl, cream the butter and margarine with the honey until smooth. Beat in the egg until well combined. Then add the applesauce, juice concentrate, lemon rind, and vanilla, beating until well blended.

Combine the dry and the wet mixtures, stirring just enough to combine. Bake for 40 minutes. Cool and frost. Sprinkle nuts over top.

Yield: 9 servings

# Maple Pecan Cake

⧫◆⧫◆⧫◆⧫◆⧫◆⧫◆⧫◆⧫◆⧫◆⧫◆⧫◆⧫◆⧫◆⧫◆⧫◆⧫◆⧫◆⧫◆⧫◆⧫◆⧫◆⧫◆⧫◆⧫◆⧫◆⧫◆⧫◆⧫◆⧫◆

⅔ cup pure maple syrup
⅓ cup apple juice concentrate
2 tablespoons butter, softened
2 tablespoons margarine, softened
1 egg
1 cup plain lowfat yogurt
1 cup whole wheat pastry flour
½ cup all-purpose flour
1½ teaspoons baking powder
½ teaspoon baking soda
¼ teaspoon salt
1 teaspoon ginger
¼ cup wheat germ
¼ cup oat flour
½ cup finely chopped pecans
Creamy Cheese Topping (page 136)
Maple syrup to taste

Preheat the oven to 375° F. Grease and flour a 9-inch square pan.

Blend the ⅔ cup maple syrup, juice concentrate, butter, and margarine. Beat in the egg.

Sift together the flours with the baking powder, baking soda, salt, and ginger. Stir in the wheat germ and oat flour. Add these dry ingredients to the syrup mixture alternately with the yogurt. Stir in the pecans.

Bake for 40 minutes. Prepare the topping, adding maple syrup to taste, and spread over the cooled cake.

Yield: 9 servings

# Marbled Spice Layer Cake

*This cake is beautiful with dark, spicy marbling. It is somewhat complicated to make and assemble, but the results are well worth the effort.*

1 cup sifted all-purpose flour
1 cup whole wheat pastry flour
2 ½ teaspoons baking powder
½ teaspoon baking soda
½ teaspoon salt
½ cup wheat germ
¼ cup oat flour
¼ cup vegetable oil
3 tablespoons margarine
3 large eggs
¾ cup apple juice concentrate
¼ cup plain lowfat yogurt

⅓ cup nonfat dry milk powder
2 tablespoons dark molasses
1 teaspoon cinnamon
½ teaspoon cloves
½ teaspoon nutmeg
1 cup apricot preserves or Apricot Glaze
   (page 140)
Milk and Honey Glaze or
   Lemon Yogurt Glaze (page 139)

Preheat the oven to 350° F. Grease and flour a 10-inch tube pan.

Sift together the flours, baking powder, baking soda, and salt; stir in wheat germ and oat flour. Set aside.

With an electric mixer, beat the oil, margarine, and eggs at high speed for about 3 minutes.

Combine the juice concentrate, yogurt, and dry milk powder. Add alternately to the egg mixture with the dry ingredients. Divide the batter in half.

Combine the molasses and spices and blend them into half the batter. Spoon the two batters into the pan in alternate spoonfuls. Cut through the batter several times with a knife or spatula to create a marbled effect.

Bake for 1 hour and 10 minutes, or until the cake springs back when the top is lightly touched with a finger. Cool on wire rack for 10 minutes; remove from pan and cool completely.

Using toothpicks, mark off three even, horizontal divisions on the side of cake. With a serrated knife, slice the cake into three layers, resting the knife on toothpicks as a guide.

Spread the bottom and middle layers with apricot preserves or glaze filling and reassemble the cake. Spoon the glaze over the top.

Yield: 12 servings

# *Classic Sponge Cake*

❖►❖►❖►❖►❖►❖►❖►❖►❖►❖►❖►❖►❖►❖►❖►❖►❖►❖►❖►❖►❖►❖►❖►❖►❖►❖►❖►❖►❖►❖►

**5 eggs, at room temperature, separated**
**¾ teaspoon cream of tartar**
**3 tablespoons white grape juice concentrate**
**1 tablespoon vanilla extract**
**¼ teaspoon almond extract**
**¼ cup water**
**¾ cup sifted all-purpose flour**
**¼ cup oat flour**
**¼ teaspoon baking soda**

Preheat the oven to 325° F. Lightly grease the bottom only of an 8-inch tube pan. Beat the egg whites and cream of tartar until stiff, set aside.

In a mixing bowl, beat the egg yolks, juice concentrate, extracts, and water for 3 minutes. Combine the flours and baking soda and fold into the egg yolk mixture. Fold the egg whites into the yolk mixture, blending in the first half thoroughly, the second half lightly.

Spoon into the pan and cut into it to release any air bubbles. Bake for 50 minutes or until well browned. Turn the pan upside down over a rack and allow it to cool completely.

Yield: 12 servings

# Simple Sponge Cake

4 eggs
½ cup sugar
¼ teaspoon salt
2 teaspoons vanilla extract or light rum
¾ cup skim or 2% lowfat milk
½ cup orange juice concentrate
1 tablespoon lemon juice
2 tablespoons butter
1 cup sifted all-purpose flour
¼ cup sifted whole wheat pastry flour
¼ cup sifted soy flour
2 teaspoons baking powder
½ cup oat flour

Preheat the oven to 350° F. Grease and flour a 9-inch square pan.

In a bowl, beat the eggs until light. Beat in the sugar, salt, and vanilla. Set aside.

Combine the milk, juice concentrate, and lemon juice in a saucepan. Heat to boiling. Add the butter and allow it to melt. The mixture will look curdled, but this doesn't matter.

Sift the first three flours with the baking powder. Stir in the oat flour. Beat the hot liquid into the egg mixture and quickly beat in the dry ingredients until just combined.

Bake for 35 minutes. Cool. Frost or serve plain with fruit or sauce.

Yield: 9 to 12 servings

49

# Orange Sponge Cake

*Here is a traditional sponge cake, enhanced with the extra nutrition of orange juice, nonfat milk powder, and oat flour. The customary topping for this cake is powdered sugar sifted lightly over the top.*

**6 eggs, separated**
**1 cup sifted all-purpose flour**
**¼ teaspoon salt**
**½ cup oat flour**
**¼ cup nonfat dry milk powder**
**¾ cup sugar, divided**
**6 tablespoons orange juice concentrate**
**1 tablespoon freshly grated orange rind**
**Powdered sugar**

In the large bowl of an electric mixer, let the egg whites come to room temperature; it will take about 1 hour.

Sift the all-purpose flour with the salt. Stir in the oat flour and dry milk. Set aside.

With the mixer at medium speed, beat the egg whites until foamy. Increase the speed and gradually beat in ¼ cup of the sugar, 1 tablespoon at a time, beating well after each addition. Beat until stiff. Set aside.

Preheat the oven to 350° F. Oil the bottom of a 10-inch tube pan.

In the small electric mixer bowl, using the same beaters, beat the egg yolks at high speed until very thick and lemon colored. This takes about 3 minutes; do not underbeat. Gradually beat in the remaining ½ cup sugar; continue beating until the mixture is smooth.

At low speed, blend the dry ingredients and juice concentrate alternately into the egg yolk mixture, beginning and ending with the dry ingredients. Add the orange rind. With a whisk or rubber scraper, using an under-and-over motion, gently fold the yolk mixture into the egg whites.

Bake for 35 to 40 minutes. Put on wire rack to cool for 30 minutes. Run a spatula around edge of cake and tube and invert the cake onto a rack. Turn right side up onto a serving plate. Sift powdered sugar over the top.

Yield: 12 servings

## *Variation*

**Orange Walnut Sponge Cake.** Stir in 1 teaspoon grated lemon rind with the orange rind, then fold in ½ cup finely chopped walnuts before adding the mixture to the egg whites.

Serve with warm Orange Sauce (page 147).

# Rum Sponge Cake

**Cake**

2 eggs

¾ cup sugar

¼ cup all-purpose flour

¼ cup whole wheat pastry flour

1 teaspoon baking powder

¼ teaspoon salt

2 tablespoons nonfat dry milk powder

1 teaspoon vanilla extract

½ cup skim or 2% lowfat milk

2 tablespoons orange juice concentrate

1 tablespoon butter

**Syrup**

½ cup light honey

½ cup water

¼ cup light rum

Preheat the oven to 375° F. Grease and flour a 9-inch springform pan.

Beat the eggs until foamy. At highest speed, gradually beat in the sugar, until very thick. Sift together the flours, baking powder, and salt; stir in the dry milk powder. Add these ingredients to the egg mixture; stir in the vanilla.

In a saucepan, combine the milk, concentrate, and butter; bring to a boil. Stir quickly into the batter. Bake for 30 minutes.

Boil honey and water 3 minutes. Cool for 10 minutes; stir in the rum. After the cake has cooled for 10 minutes, invert it onto a serving plate and pierce deeply several times with a fork. Pour the warm syrup over the top and serve. Voilà! baba au rhum!

Yield: 8 to 10 servings

# *Passover Cake*

The potato starch, which with the eggs helps to make this cake light, is available all year-round and can be found in the ethnic (or international) foods section of the super-market.

7 eggs, separated
½ cup sugar
¼ teaspoon salt
2 tablespoons grated orange rind
1 cup mashed ripe bananas
1 tablespoon thawed orange juice
   concentrate
¾ cup sifted potato starch
Orange Sauce (page 147)

Preheat the oven to 325° F. Grease the bottom (but not the sides) of a 9-inch tube pan. In a large bowl beat the egg whites until stiff. Set aside.

Using the same beaters, beat the egg yolks until thick and lemon colored; gradually beat in the sugar. Then add the salt, orange rind, bananas, and concentrate; mix well. Stir in the potato starch. Fold the egg whites gently into the banana mixture.

Bake for 50 to 60 minutes, until the cake pulls away from the pan. Invert the pan on a rack until the cake is cool. Cut the cake in wedges and serve with the warm sauce.

Yield: 8 to 12 servings

# Banana Carob Sponge Cake

◆▸◆▸◆▸◆▸◆▸◆▸◆▸◆▸◆▸◆▸◆▸◆▸◆▸◆▸◆▸◆▸◆▸◆▸◆▸◆▸◆▸◆▸◆▸◆▸◆▸

*This moist and springy cake is very quickly and easily made. It has the special flavor combination (and potassium and calcium boost) of bananas and carob and the hidden benefits of dry milk powder and good wheat bread.*

4 eggs, separated
⅓ cup nonfat dry milk powder
¼ cup carob powder or 3 tablespoons
    cocoa
2 teaspoons almond extract
¼ cup sugar
4 ripe medium-size bananas, cut in pieces
4 slices dry whole wheat or cracked
    wheat bread
Light Whipped Topping (page 138)
    (optional)

Preheat the oven to 350° F. Grease an 8-inch tube pan.

Combine the egg yolks, dry milk powder, carob, almond extract, and sugar in a blender or food processor. Whirl at medium speed to combine. Gradually add the banana pieces and continue to blend until very smooth. Transfer the mixture to a large bowl. Make the dried bread slices into crumbs (about ¾ cup) and mix them in until well combined.

Beat the egg whites until very stiff and fold them into the batter.

Pour into the prepared pan and bake for 45 to 50 minutes. Cool thoroughly before cutting. You can serve the cake plain or with a whipped topping.

Yield: 8 servings

# Light Chocolate Chiffon Cake

*Here is a simple cake for cholesterol watchers. For a fancy topping, when the cake is cool, place a paper doily over it and sieve some powdered sugar on top.*

½ cup whole wheat pastry flour
¼ cup all-purpose flour
¼ cup sugar
¼ cup unsweetened baking cocoa
1 teaspoon baking powder
¼ teaspoon salt
4 egg whites
2 tablespoons vegetable oil
2 tablespoons honey
2 tablespoons orange or apple juice
   concentrate
1 teaspoon vanilla extract
Powdered sugar (optional)

Preheat the oven to 350° F. Oil an 8-inch square baking pan and set aside. Sift the dry ingredients and set aside.

In a large bowl, beat the egg whites until foamy, then stir in the oil, honey, juice concentrate, and vanilla. Gradually and gently stir in the reserved flour mixture. Mix only until the dry ingredients are moistened.

Pour the batter into the prepared pan; spread smooth. Bake until a tester inserted into the center of the cake comes out clean, about 20 minutes. Cool for 5 minutes. Invert onto a wire rack and remove the pan; cool completely.

Yield: 9 servings

# Apple Chiffon Cake

**Cake**

⅓ cup vegetable oil
½ cup sugar
2 large eggs
½ cup whole wheat pastry flour
¼ cup wheat germ
½ teaspoon baking powder
¼ teaspoon baking soda
¼ teaspoon salt
¼ teaspoon nutmeg
¼ teaspoon ginger
1 cup finely chopped peeled tart apple

**Topping**

2 tablespoons sugar
2 tablespoons finely chopped walnuts
½ teaspoon cinnamon

Preheat the oven to 350° F.

Combine the oil and sugar in a large bowl and beat at medium speed. Add the eggs and beat well. Combine the dry ingredients and add to the oil mixture. Beat until just blended. Stir in the apple.

Spread the batter evenly in an ungreased 9-inch square pan. Combine the topping ingredients and sprinkle over the batter. Bake for 25 to 30 minutes, or until a tester inserted in the center of the cake comes out clean. Cut into bars. Serve warm or at room temperature.

Yield: 9 servings

# Angel Food Cake

*One of my clear childhood memories is of my mother making angel food cake. She had a beautiful old white china platter—large, flat, and oval—on which she whisked the egg whites until they stood in peaks. That made a real cake. An electric beater will do the job almost as well. There are those who argue that the mix for this cake is as good as homemade. Don't you believe it. You know what you have put in the cake you make yourself.*

12 egg whites (about 1½ cups),
    at room temperature
Dash salt
1 teaspoon cream of tartar
½ cup superfine sugar
1 teaspoon vanilla extract
½ teaspoon almond extract

¾ cup all-purpose flour
2 tablespoons soy flour

Preheat the oven to 350° F.

Beat the egg whites and salt until foamy; then add the cream of tartar and the sugar, a little at a time. Beat until stiff peaks form. Add the extracts and beat a little more, until glossy.

Sift the flours together 3 times. Fold into the egg whites, a quarter at a time, until just blended.

Pour the batter into an ungreased 9-inch tube pan and bake for 50 to 60 minutes, or until a tester inserted into the center of the cake comes out clean. Invert the pan on a wire rack to cool. Remove from the pan when completely cool.

Yield: 8 to 10 servings

# *Chocolate Angel Food Cake*

*For the chocolate lovers, here is a delightful airy cake.*

1/2 cup all-purpose flour
1/4 cup whole wheat pastry flour
2 tablespoons sifted oat flour
1/4 cup unsweetened baking cocoa
1 cup sugar, divided
1/4 teaspoon salt
12 egg whites (about 1 1/2 cups), at room
    temperature
1 teaspoon cream of tartar
1 teaspoon vanilla extract

Preheat the oven to 375° F. Sift together the flours, cocoa, 1/4 cup of the sugar, and the salt.

In a large mixing bowl, beat the egg whites until foamy. Beat in the cream of tartar and then gradually beat in the remaining 3/4 cup sugar. Continue to beat until stiff peaks form. Stir in the vanilla.

Sift the flour mixture, one quarter at a time, over the beaten egg whites and fold in carefully until just blended. Pour the batter into an ungreased 9-inch tube pan, and bake for 35 to 45 minutes, or until a tester inserted into the center of the cake comes out clean. Invert the pan on a wire rack to cool. Remove from the pan when completely cooled.

Yield: 8 to 10 servings

# *Pumpkin Cake Roll*

3 eggs
½ cup sugar
2 cups pumpkin puree, well drained
1 teaspoon vanilla extract
1 teaspoon grated orange rind
½ cup all-purpose flour
¼ cup whole wheat pastry flour
1 teaspoon baking powder
2 teaspoons cinnamon
1 teaspoon ginger
¼ teaspoon nutmeg
¼ teaspoon salt
2 tablespoons powdered sugar
Creamy Filling (page 148)

Preheat the oven to 375° F. Coat a 10-inch by 14-inch pan with vegetable spray. Line with waxed paper and coat with spray. Beat the eggs on high speed for 5 minutes. Gradually add the sugar. Fold in the pumpkin, vanilla, and orange rind.

Sift together the dry ingredients, except the powdered sugar. Fold gently into the pumpkin mixture. Spread evenly in the prepared pan, and bake for 12 to 15 minutes.

Sift the powdered sugar onto a linen towel. Loosen cake from the pan, turn it out onto the towel, and peel off the paper. Starting at the narrow end, roll up the cake and towel together. Cool on a rack, seam side down.

Unroll, remove the towel, spread with the filling. Reroll immediately. Chill.

Yield: 14 servings

# *Walnut Torte*

❖❖❖❖❖❖❖❖❖❖❖❖❖❖❖❖❖❖❖❖❖❖❖❖❖❖❖❖❖❖❖❖❖❖❖❖❖❖❖❖❖❖❖

*As is true of many tortes, this recipe calls for no flour. It scores nutritional points with nuts, whole grain bread crumbs, wheat germ, and lemon rind. Be sure to use a nut grinder or blender to grind the nuts.*

5 eggs, separated
½ cup light honey
1 cup finely ground walnuts
¼ cup fine, dry whole grain bread
    crumbs
3 tablespoons wheat germ
Pinch of cloves
Pinch of mace
Grated rind of 1 lemon
Light Whipped Topping (page 138)

Preheat the oven to 350° F. Oil a 9-inch springform pan well.

Beat the egg whites until stiff; set aside.

Beat the egg yolks with the honey until well blended. Add the remaining ingredients and blend well. Fold in the egg whites lightly.

Spoon the batter into the prepared pan. Bake for about 1 hour, or until the cake springs back when lightly pressed with a finger. Cool before removing from the pan. Serve with whipped topping.

Yield: 8 servings

# Torta alle Mandorle

*This Italian torte relies on nuts and combines the delicate flavors of almonds and lemon. It calls for very little flour and no shortening at all (except for greasing the pan).*

1 tablespoon butter
4 eggs, separated
¼ cup sugar
½ cup very finely chopped almonds
¼ cup all-purpose flour
¼ cup oat flour
½ teaspoon baking powder
Grated rind of 1 lemon
Powdered sugar

Preheat the oven to 350° F. Use the butter to grease a 9-inch springform pan; then dust it with flour.

Beat the egg whites until stiff. Set aside.

Beat the egg yolks, adding the sugar gradually, until light. Combine the almonds, flours, baking powder, and lemon rind; stir into the egg yolk mixture. Using a metal spoon, fold in the egg whites.

Pour the batter into the prepared pan, and bake for 35 minutes. Cool on a wire rack. Dust the top with powdered sugar.

Yield: 6 to 8 servings

# *Torta di Pere alla Paesana*

❖❖ ❖❖ ❖❖ ❖❖ ❖❖ ❖❖ ❖❖ ❖❖ ❖❖ ❖❖ ❖❖ ❖❖ ❖❖ ❖❖ ❖❖ ❖❖ ❖❖ ❖❖ ❖❖ ❖❖ ❖❖ ❖❖ ❖❖ ❖❖ ❖❖ ❖❖

*Another Italian torte, this one goes in the category of country cooking. Do not peel the pears and you will get the full nutritional benefit from the fruit.*

1 tablespoon butter
½ cup fine, dry whole wheat bread crumbs
2 eggs
¼ cup apple or white grape juice
    concentrate
¼ cup sugar
Pinch of salt
3 tablespoons dry milk powder
1 cup all-purpose flour
¼ cup whole wheat flour
¼ cup oat flour
2 pounds fresh pears
2 teaspoons lemon juice

Preheat the oven to 350° F. Grease a 9-inch layer pan with the butter, sprinkle with the bread crumbs, turn upside down to get rid of loose crumbs. Set aside.

Beat the eggs and juice concentrate together; beat in the sugar and salt. Then stir in the milk powder and the flours.

Cut the pears in half, remove the cores, and cut into thin slices, no longer than 1 inch. Sprinkle with lemon juice. Add to the batter and mix well.

Pour the batter into the prepared pan, level off the top, and bake on an upper oven shelf for 45 minutes. Cool in the pan before serving.

Yield: 6 to 8 servings

# Date and Nut Torte

*Here is a delicious torte filled with dates and nuts, which add iron, potassium, B vitamins, and vitamin E. Like many tortes, this cake has no shortening.*

**4 eggs, separated**
**½ cup sugar**
**¼ cup whole wheat pastry flour**
**1 teaspoon baking powder**
**Grated rind of 1 orange**
**1 cup chopped walnuts**
**1 cup chopped dates**
**1 teaspoon vanilla extract**
**Light Whipped Topping (page 138)**

Preheat the oven to 350° F. Grease a flat rectangular pan, 9 inches by 13 inches, or 8 by 12 inches. Set aside.

Beat the egg whites until stiff; add the sugar gradually and beat until glossy. Then beat the egg yolks and fold into the whites. Combine the flour, baking powder, and orange rind and gently stir into the egg mixture. Fold in the nuts and dates; finally stir in the vanilla.

Spoon the batter into the prepared pan and bake for about 40 minutes. Cool and serve with the topping.

Yield: 12 servings

# *Huguenot Torte*

*With a food processor to deal with the apples and nuts, this cake is very quickly made. It will puff up when it is baking and collapse when cool. Don't worry, it is supposed to be that way.*

3 eggs
1 cup sugar
5 tablespoons whole wheat flour
1 tablespoon wheat germ
1 tablespoon baking powder
¼ teaspoon salt
1½ cups chopped peeled tart apples
1½ cups chopped pecans
1½ teaspoons vanilla extract
Vanilla ice cream or Light Whipped
  Topping (page 138)

Preheat the oven to 325° F. Grease a 10-inch by 14-inch rectangular baking pan very well.

Beat the eggs with an electric mixer until very frothy and lemon colored. Add the other ingredients, except the ice cream, in the order given.

Pour the batter into the prepared pan, and bake for 45 minutes. Cool well. Cut into squares and remove from the pan with a pancake turner or spatula. Serve topped with the ice cream or whipped topping.

Yield: 12 servings

# *Swiss Carrot Torte*

*This contains no oil or shortening.*

Butter
1 heaping cup whole wheat bread crumbs
1⅔ cups unblanched almonds
1 cup grated carrots
½ teaspoon cinnamon
¼ teaspoon cloves
6 eggs
½ cup sugar
1 tablespoon grated lemon rind
2 tablespoons orange juice concentrate
1 teaspoon lemon juice
Lemon Yogurt Glaze (page 139)
   or Easy Glaze (page 138)

Preheat the oven to 350° F. Line the bottom of an 8-inch springform pan with aluminum foil; butter the bottom and sides of the pan and coat with a small amount of the bread crumbs, leaving about 1 cup.

Grind the almonds very fine in the blender or nut grinder. Mix with the carrots, bread crumbs, and spices. Beat the eggs and sugar until thick. Stir in the carrot mixture, lemon rind, juice concentrate, and lemon juice.

Bake for 1 hour. Cool. Release the springform and turn the cake upside down onto a plate. Remove the foil and refrigerate. Glaze before serving.

Yield: 6 to 8 servings

# Many Layered Fruit Torte

*Here is a fun cake for the children to make. Everyone can get into the act of adding a layer and there is no risk of disaster. In addition to all the nourishment from the dried fruits and nuts, the cake also has fresh fruits and juices, whole grains, and milk.*

1 cup quick-cooking rolled oats
3 tablespoons melted margarine
1 cup chopped dates, well packed
1 cup chopped dried apricots
1½ cups Kellogg's All-Bran cereal or
    crushed Nutri-Grain cereal or part
    cereal and part wheat germ
1 (8-ounce) can unsweetened crushed
    pineapple, very well drained
    (reserve ¼ cup juice)

1 cup raisins
1 cup finely chopped almonds
2 eggs
2 tablespoons whole wheat pastry flour
¼ cup nonfat dry milk powder
¼ cup water
¼ cup orange juice concentrate
1 cup buttermilk or skim milk
1 teaspoon vanilla extract
½ teaspoon almond extract

Assemble all the ingredients; the fruits, cereal, and nuts should go in separate bowls or cups. Preheat the oven to 325° F. Grease a 9-inch square baking pan.

    Combine the rolled oats and margarine and spread over the bottom of the pan. Pat down lightly.

Then spread evenly the following layers, in the order given: chopped dates, chopped apricots, cereal, crushed pineapple (reserve the drained juice for the topping), raisins, almonds. Press the layers down gently.

For the topping, beat the eggs. Add the flour and dry milk and beat well. Then stir in the remaining ingredients, including the $1/4$ cup pineapple juice. Pour the mixture evenly over the torte. Bake for 30 to 35 minutes, or until firm. Cool in the pan, then cut into squares. Refrigerate leftover cake or freeze for later use.

Yield: 9 to 12 servings

# *Graham Cracker Torte*

❖❖❖❖❖❖❖❖❖❖❖❖❖❖❖❖❖❖❖❖❖❖❖❖❖❖❖❖❖❖❖❖❖❖❖❖❖❖❖❖

1½ cups crushed and sifted graham
   crackers
1 teaspoon baking powder
¼ teaspoon salt
5 eggs, separated
¼ cup sugar, divided
¼ cup nonfat dry milk powder
1 cup chopped pecans
1 teaspoon vanilla extract
Light Whipped Topping (page 138) or
   Orange Sauce (page 147)

Preheat the oven to 350° F. Grease a 9-inch by 13-inch pan and set aside.

Crush the crackers (in a processor) and mix with baking powder and salt.

Beat the egg whites until stiff; then slowly add ¼ cup of the sugar, a bit at a time until the egg whites are glossy. Set aside.

With the same beaters, beat the egg yolks until thick. Slowly beat in the remaining ½ cup sugar. Stir in the graham cracker mixture, dry milk powder, chopped pecans, and vanilla. Gently fold in the egg whites.

Spoon the batter into the prepared pan, and bake for 35 to 40 minutes. Cool in the pan. Serve with the topping or sauce.

Yield: 12 servings

# *Cherry Pudding Cake*

*This is a simple cake, graced by the special flavor and color of fresh cherries.*

1½ to 2 cups pitted sour cherries
2 tablespoons honey
1 cup whole wheat pastry flour
½ cup all-purpose flour
2½ teaspoons baking powder
¼ teaspoon salt
½ cup oat flour
3 tablespoons butter, softened
¼ cup honey
1 large egg
1 cup skim or 2% lowfat milk
Vanilla ice cream or Light Whipped
    Topping (page 138)

Preheat the oven to 350° F.

Place the cherries and their juice in an 8-inch square glass baking pan or dish. Drizzle the honey over them. Sift together the dry ingredients, except the oat flour; stir it in. Cream the butter with the honey and egg, beating well. Add the dry ingredients alternately with the milk.

Pour the batter over the cherries and bake for 50 minutes. Serve very warm with the ice cream or whipped topping.

Yield: 6 to 8 servings

69

# Pineapple Upside-Down Cake

*This variation on an old favorite has no sugar and less butter and the benefits of whole grains and unsweetened pineapple.*

**Fruit Layer**
1 (8-ounce) can sliced pineapple rings, in unsweetened juice
1 tablespoon unsweetened frozen pineapple or pineapple orange juice concentrate
¼ teaspoon cinnamon or nutmeg
1 teaspoon cornstarch
1 tablespoon butter

**Cake Layer**
2 tablespoons butter, softened
2 tablespoons margarine, softened
2 tablespoons honey
1 large egg
1 teaspoon vanilla extract
½ cup unsweetened pineapple juice
3 tablespoons skim or 2% lowfat milk
½ cup all-purpose flour
½ cup whole wheat flour
½ cup oat flour
2 tablespoons nonfat dry milk powder
2 teaspoons baking powder

To prepare the fruit layer, drain the juice from the canned pineapple into a small saucepan. Save the pineapple slices for later. Add the juice concentrate, spice, and cornstarch and mix well. Bring to a boil over medium heat, stirring constantly. Boil for 1 minute. Remove from heat and stir in the butter. Pour the syrup into an 8-inch square baking pan and arrange the pineapple slices on top, cutting to fill in empty places. Set aside. Preheat the oven to 350° F.

To make the cake, beat the butter and margarine with the honey and egg until creamy. Add the vanilla, pineapple juice, and milk; beat thoroughly. Combine the dry ingredients and stir them in.

Spread the batter over the pineapple and smooth the top. Bake for about 45 minutes, or until the cake comes away from the side of the pan and a tester inserted in the center of the cake comes out clean. Run a spatula around the edges of the cake to loosen and immediately turn upside down onto a plate. Serve warm.

Yield: 6 to 9 servings

## Variations

**Cranberry Upside-Down Cake.** For the bottom layer, use 2 tablespoons melted butter mixed with ½ cup firmly packed brown sugar; spread 2 cups cranberries over this. For the cake, substitute ½ cup orange juice for the pineapple juice.

**Peach Upside-Down Cake.** For the bottom layer, use 2 tablespoons melted butter mixed with ⅓ cup firmly packed brown sugar; cover with fresh or canned drained peach halves (round side down) or slices. For the cake, substitute ½ cup orange juice or apricot nectar for the pineapple juice.

# *Rhubaba*

Here is another upside-down cake, somewhat fancier than Pineapple Upside-Down cake and its variations. The cake part is a sponge cake and the rhubarb is flavored with sherry. This makes a wonderful party dessert.

**Fruit Layer**
1 tablespoon butter
1 tablespoon light margarine
½ cup brown sugar
2 cups diced rhubarb
¼ cup dry sherry

**Cake Layer**
3 eggs, separated
1 teaspoon lemon juice
½ cup sugar

¼ cup orange or apple juice concentrate
¼ cup water
½ cup all-purpose flour
¼ cup whole wheat pastry flour
1½ teaspoons baking powder
¼ teaspoon salt
¼ cup oat flour
Light Whipped Topping (page 138)

Melt the butter and margarine in a large (at least 10 inches in diameter), round flat baking pan; stir in the brown sugar. Top evenly with the rhubarb and drizzle the sherry over the top. Set aside.

Preheat the oven to 325° F.

Beat the egg whites until stiff; set aside. In a large bowl, beat the egg yolks and lemon juice until thick; then gradually add the sugar and beat until light. Heat the juice concentrate and water together until hot and slowly stir it in.

Sift together the dry ingredients, except the oat flour. Blend in the oat flour and add all the dry ingredients slowly to the egg yolk mixture, stirring gently until well combined. Fold in the egg whites.

Spoon the batter evenly over the rhubarb. Bake for 1 hour, or until a tester inserted into the center of the cake comes out clean. Remove from the oven and let stand for 5 minutes. Loosen the sides and invert the cake onto a serving plate. Cut into wedges and serve warm with the whipped topping.

Yield: 8 to 10 servings

# Magic Lemon Pudding Cake

*This recipe has come down through many generations. The magic is that you mix everything together and while the cake is baking, it separates into a spongelike top and a saucelike bottom. This is a perfect dessert for lemon lovers.*

1 tablespoon butter
¼ cup sugar
2 tablespoons light honey
2 tablespoons all-purpose flour
1 tablespoon nonfat dry milk powder
Juice and grated rind of 2 lemons
2 eggs, separated
1 cup skim or 2% lowfat milk

Preheat the oven to 350° F. Grease 6 custard cups or one 3-cup or 4-cup baking dish (a small soufflé dish is perfect) and set in a pan containing about 1 inch of hot water.

Cream the butter with the sugar and honey until light. Add the flour, dry milk, lemon juice and rind, egg yolks, and milk. Beat well until smooth.

Beat the egg whites until stiff and gently fold into the lemon mixture. Pour the batter into the prepared dish(es) and bake the individual desserts for 30 minutes, the single dish for 40 minutes. Serve chilled.

Yield: 6 servings

# *Shortcake Slices*

*This cake is sliced into individual servings, giving you the option of offering several different toppings.*

1 large egg, separated
½ cup skim milk
¼ cup light honey
½ teaspoon vanilla extract
1 cup whole wheat pastry flour
2 tablespoons oat flour
1 teaspoon baking powder
¼ teaspoon baking soda
¼ teaspoon salt
2 tablespoons butter
2 tablespoons vegetable oil
Fresh Strawberry Sauce or Fresh
    Currant Sauce (page 143)

Preheat the oven to 350° F. Grease a 5-inch by 9-inch loaf pan.

Beat the egg white until stiff and set aside. With the same beaters, beat the egg yolk in a small bowl. Add the milk, honey, and vanilla, beating until well blended.

Measure the dry ingredients into a large bowl and mix them together. Cut in the butter and oil until the mixture is crumbly. Stir in the milk mixture and blend well. Gently fold in the egg white.

Bake for 40 minutes. Cool for 10 minutes, then remove from the pan. Cool completely. Cut into slices and cover with the fruit sauce of your choosing.

Yield: 12 servings

# Blueberry-Lemon Shortcake

*This takes some time but it is well worth it. Here is a high-protein, high-calcium treat.*

**Shortcake**
1 cup whole wheat pastry flour
1 cup all-purpose flour
2 tablespoons sugar
2 teaspoons baking powder
½ teaspoon baking soda
⅛ teaspoon salt
¼ cup margarine
1 cup plain lowfat yogurt
1 egg, beaten

**Filling**
2 tablespoons cornstarch
½ cup skim milk

2 tablespoons light honey
½ teaspoon vanilla extract
1 cup lowfat lemon yogurt
2 teaspoons grated lemon rind
1½ cups fresh blueberries

Preheat the oven to 450° F. Grease a 9-inch round pan or 8-inch square pan with oil.

Combine the dry ingredients. Cut in the margarine until the mixture resembles coarse meal. Add the plain yogurt and beaten egg. Stir until just moistened. Turn out onto a board and knead gently for 1 minute. Pat evenly into the prepared pan and bake for 15 minutes. Cool for 10 minutes. Remove from the pan and split into two layers.

While the shortcake is baking, prepare the

filling. Combine the cornstarch, milk, and honey in a small saucepan. Bring to boil, stirring, over medium-high heat. Reduce the heat and cook, stirring constantly, until thickened. Cool, stir in the vanilla and lemon yogurt and rind.

To assemble, spread half of the filling over the bottom of the shortcake, top with half of the blueberries. Repeat for the top layer. Cut into squares or wedges to serve.

Yield: 6 to 8 servings

# Cottage Pudding

❖❖❖❖❖❖❖❖❖❖❖❖❖❖❖❖❖❖❖❖❖❖❖❖❖❖❖❖❖❖❖❖❖❖❖❖❖❖❖❖❖❖

*Here is an old favorite, a very plain and simple cake to be served with crushed fresh fruit, fruit sauces, or, traditionally, lemon sauce.*

¼ cup sugar
2 tablespoons butter, softened
2 tablespoons margarine, softened
1 egg
1 teaspoon vanilla extract
1 cup sifted all-purpose flour
½ cup sifted whole wheat pastry flour
2 teaspoons baking powder
¼ teaspoon salt
2 tablespoons nonfat dry milk powder
½ cup apple or white grape juice
　　concentrate

Lemon Sauce (page 146) or Applesauce
　　Topping (page 145)

Preheat the oven to 400° F. Grease an 8-inch square pan.

Cream the sugar with the butter and margarine until creamy. Beat in the egg and vanilla.

Sift the flours with the baking powder and salt. Stir in the milk powder. Add the dry ingredients to the creamed mixture in 3 parts, alternately with the juice concentrate. Beat the batter until it is smooth after each addition.

Pour the batter into the prepared pan and bake for about 25 minutes. Cool before serving. Cut the cake into squares and cover with the Lemon Sauce or Applesauce Topping or any of the fruit sauces in the last chapter.

Yield: 9 servings

# Peach Almond Cake

*Another family favorite cake with fresh fruit, this one is very simple and very quickly made.*

Ripe fresh peach halves, peeled
1 tablespoon butter
1 tablespoon margarine
¼ cup sugar
1 large egg, beaten
¼ cup whole wheat pastry flour
¼ cup all-purpose flour
¼ teaspoon baking powder
Dash of salt
¼ teaspoon almond extract

Preheat the oven to 400° F.

Arrange the peach halves in a shallow 1-quart baking dish or 9-inch layer cake pan or pie pan. Mix the remaining ingredients together and spoon on top. Bake for 25 minutes. Serve warm or at room temperature.

Yield: 6 to 8 servings

# Blueberry Cake with Vanilla Sauce

This cake is wonderful, especially when blue-berries are in season. If you use frozen berries, do not thaw them before adding to the batter.

**Cake**
1 egg
⅓ cup light honey or pure maple syrup
1 cup all-purpose flour
¼ cup whole wheat pastry flour
1 cup fresh or frozen blueberries
2 teaspoons baking powder
¼ teaspoon baking soda
¼ teaspoon salt
¼ cup wheat germ
½ cup skim milk or buttermilk
3 tablespoons vegetable oil
1 teaspoon vanilla extract
1 teaspoon grated lemon rind

**Vanilla Sauce**
¼ cup light honey
2 tablespoons white grape juice concentrate
2 tablespoons cornstarch
1½ cups boiling water
1 tablespoon butter
1 tablespoon vanilla extract
Dash of nutmeg

To make the cake, preheat the oven to 400° F. Grease a 5-inch by 9-inch loaf pan. Line the bottom with waxed paper and grease again.

Beat the egg and gradually add the honey.

Measure the flours, remove a little, and mix it with the berries. Sift together the flours, baking powder, baking soda, and salt. Stir in the wheat germ. Add the dry ingredients to the

egg mixture alternately with the milk. Stir in the oil, vanilla, and lemon rind. Mix until smooth. Fold in the blueberries.

Pour the batter into the prepared pan. Bake for 30 minutes. Serve warm with the sauce.

To make the sauce, combine the honey, juice concentrate, and cornstarch in a small saucepan. Stir in the boiling water and cook, stirring, until thickened and clear. Stir in the butter. Cool somewhat, then stir in the vanilla and nutmeg. Serve warm.

Yield: 6 to 8 servings

## Variation

**Cranberry Cake with Vanilla Sauce.** Substitute 1/3 cup orange juice concentrate for the milk and 1 1/2 cups coarsely chopped cranberries for the blueberries. You can also add 1 tablespoon grated orange rind to the cake batter, if you wish.

# *Sunny Squares*

❖❖❖❖❖❖❖❖❖❖❖❖❖❖❖❖❖❖❖❖❖❖❖❖❖❖❖❖❖❖❖❖❖❖❖❖❖❖❖❖❖❖

**3 tablespoons light margarine, softened**
**2 large eggs**
**½ cup unsweetened pineapple orange juice concentrate**
**1 tablespoon orange juice concentrate**
**1 tablespoon lemon juice**
**½ cup all-purpose flour**
**½ cup oat flour**
**½ teaspoon baking powder**
**¼ teaspoon baking soda**
**2 cups unsweetened pineapple juice**
**¼ cup cornstarch**
**2 tablespoons toasted flaked coconut (optional)**
**1 cup orange segments, drained**

Preheat the oven to 325° F. Lightly oil a 9-inch square baking pan. Beat together the margarine and eggs. Mix in the juice concentrates and lemon juice. Combine the dry ingredients and beat into the liquid mixture.

Bake for 20 minutes. Do not remove the cake from the pan. Cool.

To prepare the topping, mix together the juice and cornstarch. Cook over medium heat, stirring constantly, until thickened. Remove from heat and cool. Pour the mixture over the cake, sprinkle with the coconut, and garnish with the orange segments or 2 cups fresh blueberries. Refrigerate until firm. Cut into squares.

Yield: 9 servings

# 5
# *Cheesecakes*

❖►❖►❖►❖►❖►❖►❖►❖►❖►❖►❖►❖►❖►❖►❖►❖►❖►❖►❖►❖►❖►❖►❖►❖►❖►❖►❖►

As its name says, this cake traditionally is made with cream cheese, cottage cheese, and/or ricotta cheese. Various forms of cheesecake have been around for centuries. Here in the States such cakes generally come from two ethnic backgrounds, the Jewish and the Italian. A Jewish cheesecake has a very smooth cream cheese filling, whereas an Italian cheesecake is made with ricotta; both may have a graham cracker or pastry crust.

Cheesecakes are very popular and are truly worthy of this popularity. Unfortunately, the traditional type, made with cream cheese, is very high in fat. The cheesecakes here aim to remove that problem without sacrificing the wonderful taste and texture of the original. If your idea of a healthy cake is one that will fatten up the poor eater or build up the athlete in your family, then use cream cheese in any of these recipes, or try the variation of the Classic Cheesecake (page 87) called Sam's Cheesecake. For the rest of us, however, avoiding so much fat is the healthiest way.

The nutritional benefits of cheesecakes are clear. Although cream cheese and cottage cheese (as "fresh" cheeses) are poor sources of calcium, they contain all the other benefits of milk—high protein, vitamins A and D, the B vitamins. While the fat content of cream cheese is very high (70 percent or more) and that of part skim ricotta is moderately high, cottage cheese (especially lowfat) and farmer cheese have a low fat content. And don't forget that the commercial lowfat cream cheese, which goes under the name of Neufchâtel, can be used instead of cream cheese. Because of additives, however, I tend to avoid it.

# *Classic Cheesecake*

‣‣‣‣‣‣‣‣‣‣‣‣‣‣‣‣‣‣‣‣‣‣‣‣‣‣‣‣‣‣‣‣‣‣‣‣‣‣‣‣‣‣‣‣‣‣‣‣‣‣‣‣‣‣‣‣‣

*This is the cheesecake I make the most often. Although it does not have the completely smooth texture of a cake made with cream cheese, its taste is hard to beat.*

**Graham Cracker Crust or
    Oat Crust (page 96)**
**11 ounces farmer cheese**
**¾ cup creamed cottage cheese**
**½ cup sugar**
**3 eggs**
**1 tablespoon white grape juice
    concentrate**
**1 teaspoon lemon juice**
**1 teaspoon vanilla extract**
**Grated nutmeg**

Preheat the oven to 350° F. Prepare the crust and press onto the bottom and sides of a 9-inch springform pan or an 8-inch by 10-inch rectangular pan. Bake the crust for about 10 minutes. Remove from oven and set aside. Beat the farmer cheese and cottage cheese at high speed until very smooth. Add the sugar gradually, beating continually. Reduce the mixer speed and add the eggs, one at a time. Beat in the juice concentrate, lemon juice, and vanilla until well blended. Pour the filling into the prepared crust and return the cake to the oven. Bake for 35 to 40 minutes, or until firm. Cool completely and grate fresh nutmeg over the top. Chill thoroughly before serving.

Yield: 8 to 10 servings

### Variations

**Peaches and Cream Cake.** Prepare and bake the cheesecake as above, using a rectangular pan. Do not remove it from the pan. When it is cool, arrange 2 cups fresh sliced peaches over the top and cover with Orange Glaze (page 140). Chill thoroughly before serving directly from the pan.

**Sam's Cheesecake.** Add 2 tablespoons butter or margarine to the crust. In the cheese layer, substitute 11 ounces cream cheese for the farmer cheese, increase the grape juice concentrate to 2 tablespoons, and add 2 tablespoons dry milk powder.

**Italian Ricotta Cake.** Prepare your favorite pastry crust and place in a 9-inch or 10-inch pie plate; do not bake it in advance. Substitute 2½ cups ricotta (part skim or "lite," if possible) for the farmer cheese and cottage cheese. Add 2 tablespoons slivered toasted almonds, 1 tablespoon minced citron, and 2 teaspoons freshly grated orange rind. Bake for about 45 minutes. After the cake is cool, sprinkle powdered sugar over the top and serve from the pan.

# Yogurt Cheesecake

*This basic cheesecake combines the nutrition and flavor of yogurt, honey, and lemon juice and rind.*

Wheat Germ Crust or Wheat Germ
    Crumb Crust (page 96)
3 eggs, separated
1½ cups plain lowfat yogurt
1 teaspoon vanilla extract
1 tablespoon lemon juice
Grated rind of 1 lemon
¼ cup honey
¼ teaspoon salt
¼ cup whole wheat pastry flour or
    oat flour
1½ cups creamed cottage cheese

Pat the crust into the bottom of a 9-inch springform or round cake pan. Preheat the oven to 350° F.

Beat the egg whites until stiff. Set aside.

Combine the yogurt, egg yolks, and all the remaining ingredients in a blender or food processor. Whirl until very smooth. Pour the mixture into a bowl and fold in the egg whites gently.

Pour the mixture into the prepared crust. Bake for 35 to 40 minutes, or until the center of the cake is firm. Run a knife around the edge of the pan to loosen the cake from the sides. Cool completely before removing from the pan and chill thoroughly before serving.

Yield: 8 to 10 servings

# Tofu Cheesecake

Tofu is a processed food made from soybeans, and one where the processing makes a richer source of calcium than the original product; also the iron in tofu is three times more available than that in soybeans. In addition, tofu supplies complete proteins, almost to the extent that milk does. Just be sure it is fresh.

Graham Cracker Crust (page 96)
1¼ pounds tofu
1 cup lowfat cottage cheese or 8 ounces
    farmer cheese
1 egg
¼ cup light honey
3 tablespoons vegetable oil
Juice of 1 lemon
1 teaspoon vanilla extract
¼ teaspoon salt
1 tablespoon cornstarch dissolved in 2
    tablespoons apple juice concentrate,
    thawed but cool

Prepare the crust and press into an 8-inch square pan or a 9-inch springform pan. Preheat the oven to 350° F.

In a large bowl, mash the tofu thoroughly with the cottage cheese. Blend the remaining ingredients in a blender or food processor. Stir this into the tofu mixture and blend (in two batches) until very smooth.

Pour the filling into the prepared crust and bake for 30 to 40 minutes, until golden and firm. Cool before removing from the pan and chill thoroughly before serving.

Yield: 8 to 10 servings

# Eggless Tofu Cheesecake

*Honey Oat Crust*
1½ cups quick-cooking rolledoats
2 tablespoons honey
¼ cup vegetable oil

*Cheesecake*
1½ pounds tofu
⅓ cup light honey
2 tablespoons lemon juice
¼ cup vegetable oil
¼ cup skimmed milk
1½ teaspoons vanilla extract
1 teaspoon cinnamon
½ teaspoon nutmeg
¼ teaspoon salt
**Orange Glaze or Apricot Glaze (page 140)**

To prepare the crust, mix the honey with the oil and pour over the oats. Press into an 8-inch square pan. Bake at 325° F. for 10 minutes. Cool.

To make the cheesecake filling, combine all the ingredients, except the glaze, in a large bowl. Blend, half at a time, in a blender or food processor until very smooth. Pour into the prepared crust and return to the oven for about 50 minutes, or until the top feels slightly firm. Cool before removing from the pan. Chill thoroughly before serving. Cover with the glaze or a fruit sauce.

Yield: 8 to 9 servings

# *Apricot Cheesecake*

*Here is a cheesecake with the added nutrition of apricots, orange juice, and yogurt.*

**Wheat Germ Crust (page 96)**
**1 cup dried apricots**
**½ cup orange juice**
**1 cup lowfat cottage cheese or 8 ounces farmer cheese**
**1 cup plain lowfat yogurt**
**4 eggs**
**2 teaspoons freshly grated orange rind**
**Dash of salt**
**2 tablespoons whole wheat pastry flour or oat flour**

Prepare the crust and pat it into a 10-inch pie pan; do not bake.

Combine the apricots and orange juice in a small saucepan and boil gently for 5 minutes. Remove from the heat and cool.

Preheat the oven to 350° F.

Combine cottage cheese and yogurt in a blender and process until smooth. Blend in the eggs, one at a time.

Add the cooked apricot mixture to the mixture in the blender and whirl until smooth. Fold in the orange rind, salt, and flour.

Pour the filling into the prepared crust and bake for 45 minutes. Cool, then cover, and chill thoroughly before serving from the pan.

Yield 10 to 12 servings

# Autumn Apple Cheesecake

*The tart apples and chopped nuts added to the smooth cheesecake makes a tasty and nutritious combination, perfect for a crisp fall evening.*

**Graham Cracker Crust (page 96)**
**1 teaspoon cinnamon, divided**
**8 ounces farmer cheese**
**1 cup cottage cheese**
**½ cup sugar, divided**
**2 eggs**
**1 teaspoon vanilla extract**
**4 cups thinly sliced peeled tart apples**
**½ cup chopped pecans**

Preheat the oven to 350° F. Prepare the crust, adding to it ½ teaspoon of the cinnamon. Press on the bottom and sides of a 9-inch springform pan. Bake for 10 minutes.

Combine the farmer cheese, cottage cheese, and ¼ cup of the sugar, beating until well blended. Add the eggs, one at a time, beating well after each addition. Stir in the vanilla. Pour over the crust.

Toss the apples with remaining ¼ cup sugar, mixed with the remaining ½ teaspoon cinnamon. Spoon this over the cheese layer; sprinkle with pecans. Return the cake to the oven and bake for 65 to 70 minutes. Cool the cake before removing it from the pan. Chill thoroughly before serving.

Yield 8 to 10 servings

## Variation

**Spicy Autumn Apple Cheesecake.** Prepare the crust as before and bake. In a heavy skillet, cook the apples with the $\frac{1}{4}$ cup sugar, 2 tablespoons margerine, and $\frac{1}{4}$ teaspoon each of cinnamon, cardamon, nutmeg, and cloves. Stir frequently and cook just until the apples start to carmelize. Arrange the apples over the baked crust and sprinkle the nuts over them. Then prepare the cheese layer and pour it over the apples. Reduce the oven temperature to 325° F. and bake for 65 minutes, or until lightly browned. Turn off the oven and leave the cheesecake there for 1 hour with the oven door slightly opened. Cool on a wire rack and remove from the pan. Chill for several hours before serving.

# *Banana Peanut Cheesecake*

*◆▸◆▸◆▸◆▸◆▸◆▸◆▸◆▸◆▸◆▸◆▸◆▸◆▸◆▸◆▸◆▸◆▸◆▸◆▸◆▸◆▸◆▸◆▸◆▸◆▸◆▸◆▸◆▸◆▸◆▸◆▸◆▸◆▸◆▸◆▸◆▸*

*This cheesecake combines the special flavor and high nutrition of bananas and peanuts with a touch of chocolate.*

Oat Crust (page 96)
½ cup semisweet chocolate bits, melted
8 ounces Neufchâtel cream cheese
8 ounces farmer cheese
1 cup creamed cottage cheese
3 tablespoons light honey
½ cup mashed ripe bananas
3 eggs
½ cup chopped peanuts

Preheat the oven to 350° F. Prepare the crust, using only 3 tablespoons brown sugar. Press it onto the bottom and partly up the sides of a 9-inch springform pan. Bake for 10 minutes. Cool slightly and gently spread the melted chocolate bits over the warm crust. Set aside.

Using an electric mixer at medium to high speed, combine the cheeses, honey, and bananas, blending well. Add the eggs, one at a time, beating well after each addition.

Pour the filling over the prepared crust, sprinkle the peanuts over the top, and return to the oven. Bake for about 40 minutes. Cool the cake before removing from the pan. Chill well before serving.

Yield: 8 to 12 servings

# Pumpkin Cheesecake

*Here is a smooth, delicious alternative to pumpkin pie. Make your own pumpkin puree, if you possibly can, and drain it well.*

**Oat Crust or Oat and Nut Crust (page 96)**
**8 ounces farmer cheese or Neufchâtel cream cheese**
**1 cup creamed cottage cheese**
**¼ cup orange juice concentrate**
**2 tablespoons light honey**
**2 eggs**
**2 cups pumpkin puree**
**1 teaspoon cinnamon**
**¼ teaspoon nutmeg**
**¼ teaspoon ginger**
**Dash of salt**

Preheat the oven to 350° F. Make the crust and press it on the bottom and up sides of a 9-inch springform pan. Bake and cool it while you prepare the filling.

Combine the cheeses, juice concentrate, and honey and beat at medium to high speed with an electric mixer until smooth. Add the eggs, one at a time, and beat well. Blend in the pumpkin, spices, and salt. Pour into the baked crust and return to the oven. Bake for 50 minutes. Cool, then remove from the pan. Chill thoroughly before serving.

Yield: 8 to 10 servings

# *Eggless Cheesecake*

❖►❖►❖►❖►❖►❖►❖►❖►❖►❖►❖►❖►❖►❖►❖►❖►❖►❖►❖►❖►❖►❖►❖►❖►❖►❖►❖►❖►❖►❖►

*Here it is, the cheesecake for low-calorie, lowfat, and low-cholesterol diets. It is delicious.*

1 tablespoon margarine
¼ cup graham cracker crumbs
2 cups lowfat cottage cheese
1 cup part skim ricotta cheese
2 tablespoons light honey
1 teaspoon grated lemon rind
1 teaspoon vanilla extract
2 tablespoons lemon juice
2 tablespoons orange juice
　　concentrate, cold
4 teaspoons unflavored gelatin
Freshly grated nutmeg (optional)

Grease an 8-inch round pan with margarine. Sprinkle the bottom and sides of the pan with the crumbs and set aside.

Blend the cottage cheese and ricotta in a blender until smooth. Add the honey and blend until smooth. Pour the mixture into a bowl and stir in the lemon rind and vanilla.

In a small bowl, mix the lemon juice with the juice concentrate. Sprinkle the gelatin over and let stand for 5 minutes to soften. Place the bowl over simmering water and dissolve the gelatin completely. Let it cool but not set. Stir the gelatin into the cheese mixture and pour into the prepared pan.

Refrigerate for 3 hours. Serve dusted with nutmeg or with a fruit sauce.

Yield: 6 servings

# *Skinny Cheesecake*

*This cake with eggs is a cheesecake for the serious dieter. If you dare to do so, use a very thin crust for the bottom.*

1 tablespoon plain gelatin
2 tablespoons lemon juice
½ cup hot skim milk
2½ cups lowfat cottage cheese
2 eggs, separated
¾ cup crushed ice
¼ cup orange juice or white grape juice
    concentrate (do not thaw)
1 teaspoon grated lemon rind

Soften the gelatin in the lemon juice; then stir in the hot milk and blend to dissolve completely. Combine in the blender with the cottage cheese and egg yolks. Blend at high speed for 2 minutes. Add the crushed ice and frozen juice concentrate and continue blending at high speed until completely mixed. Beat the egg whites until very stiff, then fold them into the cheese mixture along with the lemon rind.

Pour the mixture into an 8-inch mold. Chill until firm, about 24 hours. Unmold and serve, if you like, with a fresh fruit sauce.

Yield: 6 servings

# *Crusts*

### Graham Cracker Crust

Combine 1½ cups graham cracker crumbs, ¼ cup melted margarine or vegetable oil, and 3 tablespoons brown sugar or 1 tablespoon honey with a fork. Press into the pan. Bake at 350° F. for 10 minutes, or as directed.

### Oat Crust

Combine 1½ cups rolled oats, 3 tablespoons margarine, and ¼ cup brown sugar with your fingers until mixed and crumbly. Press into the pan. Bake at 350° F. for 10 minutes, or as directed.

### Oat and Nut Crust

Combine 1½ cups quick- cooking rolled oats, ½ cup finely chopped nuts, and 2 tablespoons brown sugar in a bowl. Melt 4 tablespoons margarine and mix with 2 tablespoons honey. Pour over the dry ingredients. Blend thoroughly. Press into the pan. Bake at 350° F. for about 10 minutes, or as directed.

### Wheat Germ Crust

Mix ½ cup wheat germ, ½ cup whole wheat flour, ½ teaspoon cinnamon, and 1 teaspoon freshly grated orange rind with a fork. Add 3 tablespoons vegetable oil, stirring to moisten the ingredients evenly. Press into the pan. Bake at 350° F. for 10 minutes, or as directed in the recipe.

### Wheat Germ Crumb Crust

Combine 1 cup wheat germ with ½ cup graham cracker crumbs. Mix together 3 tablespoons honey and 3 tablespoons melted margarine or vegetable oil and blend into the dry ingredients. Press into the pan. Bake at 350° F. for 10 minutes, or as directed.

# 6
# Coffee Cakes and Breakfast Cakes

For nearly twenty years of my adult life, we had a special Sunday breakfast in our family. We had muffins sometimes and pancakes very rarely. Most often we ate a breakfast cake.

Like the snacking cake, the coffee/breakfast cake is a simple cake baked in a square or rectangular pan. It often contains fruit and has a crumb topping or a light glaze on top; it usually is served warm. Many of the cakes below would make fine snacking cakes, and several snacking cakes—Apple Betty Crunch Cake, for one example—make fine coffee cakes.

In addition to their place on the breakfast menu, these cakes are the ideal choice for the morning coffee party or a special brunch.

# *Blueberry Buckle*

+>+>+>+>+>+>+>+>+>+>+>+>+>+>+>+>+>+>+>+>+>+>+>+>+>+>+>+>+>+>+>+

*Of all the coffee cakes, this one takes first prize. This cake has been a family favorite for years. If you possibly can, choose small blueberries for this treat. If you use frozen berries, be sure thay are completely thawed before you add them to the batter.*

**Cake**
2 tablespoons butter, softened
2 tablespoons margarine, softened
⅓ cup sugar
1 egg
1 cup whole wheat pastry flour
¾ cup oat flour or all-purpose flour
¼ cup wheat germ
1 teaspoon baking powder
½ teaspoon baking soda
¼ teaspoon salt
¼ cup apple or white grape juice concentrate
¼ cup buttermilk or skim milk
1 tablespoon nonfat dry milk powder
2 cups blueberries

**Topping**
2 tablespoons butter
¼ cup brown sugar
¼ cup whole wheat flour
¼ cup quick-cooking rolled oats
2 tablespoons wheat germ
½ teaspoon cinnamon

Preheat the oven to 375° F. Grease a 9-inch square pan.

Cream the butter and margarine. Add the sugar slowly and mix well. Beat in the egg.

Combine the next ingredients. Mix together the juice concentrate, buttermilk, and dry milk powder. Add the dry ingredients to the creamed mixture alternately with the liquid. Gently fold in the blueberries.

Pour the batter into the prepared pan; it will be quite thick. Gently smooth the top. Combine the topping ingredients (this is most easily done with the fingers or in a food processor) and sprinkle evenly over the top. Bake for about 35 minutes, or until the cake comes away from the sides of the pan. Cool slightly, remove from the pan. Serve warm.

Yield: 9 servings

## Variations

**Peach Buckle.** Instead of folding in the blueberries, arrange fresh (or canned, well drained) peach slices or halves (about 2½ cups) over the batter. Sprinkle the topping over and bake as above.

**Cranberry Buckle.** Increase the sugar to ½ cup in the batter, substitute orange juice concentrate for the apple, and stir in 1 tablespoon grated orange rind into the batter. Instead of folding in blueberries, sprinkle 1½ cups chopped cranberries over the top. Then sprinkle the topping over and bake as above.

# Buttermilk Crumb Cake

◆▸◆▸◆▸◆▸◆▸◆▸◆▸◆▸◆▸◆▸◆▸◆▸◆▸◆▸◆▸◆▸◆▸◆▸◆▸◆▸◆▸◆▸◆▸◆▸◆▸◆▸◆▸◆▸◆▸◆▸◆▸

½ cup all-purpose flour
½ cup oat flour
½ cup whole wheat pastry flour
½ cup rolled oats
2 tablespoons wheat germ
2 tablespoons cornmeal
½ cup brown sugar
6 tablespoons margarine, chilled
½ cup chopped nuts or soy nuts or
   2 tablespoons sesame seeds
2 tablespoons dry milk powder
1 teaspoon baking soda
½ teaspoon baking powder
¼ teaspoon salt
1 egg, well beaten
1 cup buttermilk or plain lowfat yogurt
1 teaspoon vanilla extract

½ cup raisins
¼ cup chopped dried apricots

Preheat the oven to 375° F. Grease a 9-inch by 13-inch pan. Combine the flours, oats, wheat germ, cornmeal, and brown sugar. Cut in the cold margarine. Measure out half of the mixture, mix in the nuts (or seeds), and set aside for the topping.

Stir the dry milk powder, baking soda, baking powder, and salt into the second half of the mixture and blend well. Add the remaining ingredients, beating until well mixed.

Pour into the prepared pan. Cover with the reserved crumb mixture. Bake for 30 minutes. Cool for a few minutes and cut into squares. Serve warm.

# Peach Bran Coffee Cake

*If you cannot get fresh peaches, use one 16-ounce can of sliced peaches. Drain the syrup, measure ²/₃ cup, and use instead of the concentrate and water.*

1 cup Kellogg's All-Bran cereal
¹/₃ cup white grape juice concentrate
¹/₃ cup water
1 egg
¹/₄ cup vegetable oil
1 cup whole wheat pastry flour
2¹/₂ teaspoons baking powder
¹/₄ teaspoon salt
³/₄ teaspoon cinnamon, divided
2 cups peeled, sliced fresh peaches
2 tablespoons sugar

Preheat the oven to 400° F. Grease a 9-inch square baking pan. Measure the cereal, juice concentrate, and water into a mixing bowl; let stand until the moisture is absorbed. Add the egg and oil and beat well.

Sift together the flour, baking powder, salt, and ¹/₂ teaspoon of the cinnamon. Add to the cereal; stir only until combined. Spread in the prepared pan. With a floured spoon, make grooves in the batter diagonally across the pan, about 1¹/₂ inches apart, forming a lattice.

Place the peach slices in the grooves. Combine the remaining ¹/₄ teaspoon cinnamon with the sugar and sprinkle over the top. Bake for about 30 minutes, or until browned. Cool in the pan and cut in squares to serve.

Yield: 9 servings

# *Apple Kuchen*

**Filling**
**3 cups thinly sliced apples (do not peel)**
**¼ cup chopped walnuts or pecans**
**¼ cup raisins**
**2 tablespoons sugar**
**1 teaspoon cinnamon**

**Cake**
**¼ cup vegetable oil**
**2 eggs**
**¼ cup honey**
**⅓ cup apple juice concentrate**
**2 tablespoons nonfat dry milk powder**
**1 teaspoon vanilla extract**
**1 cup whole wheat pastry flour**
**¼ cup oat flour**
**¼ cup wheat germ**
**1½ teaspoons baking powder**
**¼ teaspoon salt**

Preheat the oven to 350° F. Grease a deep 9-inch pie plate or 9-inch square baking pan.

Mix the filling ingredients and set aside.

Combine the oil, eggs, and honey and beat until well blended. Mix together the juice concentrate, milk powder, and vanilla. Combine the dry ingredients. Add them to the creamed mixture alternately with the liquid ingredients.

Spread half of the batter in the pie pan, on the bottom and up the sides. Add the filling evenly over the top and then spread the remaining batter over. Bake for 50 to 60 minutes. Serve warm.

Yield: 6 to 9 servings

# Applesauce Coffee Cake

*This recipe and Spicy Raisin Corn Bread (next page), make wonderful cornmeal cakes. They have the benefits of dried fruit, plus the nutritional boost of several whole grain, and are quickly made.*

2 cups cornmeal
1 cup whole wheat pastry flour
½ cup oat flour
½ cup rye flour
1 teaspoon baking soda
½ teaspoon salt
1 cup buttermilk
¼ cup light molasses
¼ cup apple cider
¼ cup slightly sweetened applesauce
¼ cup raisins

Preheat the oven to 350° F. Grease a 9-inch by 13-inch baking pan.

Mix the cornmeal, flours, baking soda, and salt in a large bowl. Add the buttermilk, molasses, and cider and beat with a spoon until smooth. Fold in the applesauce and raisins.

Bake for 40 minutes. Cool 10 minutes. Cut into squares and serve warm.

Yield: 12 to 15 servings

## Variation

**Applesauce Date Nut Coffee Cake.** To the dry ingredients, add 1 teaspoon each of cinnamon, allspice, and nutmeg. Substitute 1 cup dates, pitted and chopped, and 1 cup chopped walnuts for the raisins. Fold them in with the applesauce. Bake as above.

# Spicy Raisin Corn Bread

**Cake**
3/4 cup cornmeal
1/2 cup whole wheat pastry flour
1/4 cup soy flour
1/4 cup all-purpose flour
1/4 cup wheat germ
2 tablespoons sugar
1 tablespoon nutritional yeast
1 tablespoon baking powder
1/4 teaspoon salt
1 teaspoon cinnamon
1/4 teaspoon ginger
1/4 teaspoon allspice
1 cup buttermilk or skim milk
2 tablespoons vegetable oil
1 egg
1 cup raisins

**Topping**
1/4 cup brown sugar
1/4 cup quick-cooking rolled oats
3 tablespoons wheat germ
1 teaspoon cinnamon
2 tablespoons butter or margarine

Preheat the oven to 400° F. Grease a 9-inch square pan.

In a large mixing bowl, combine all the dry ingredients. Measure the buttermilk and oil into a large measuring cup, beat the egg into it, and pour over the dry ingredients. Mix quickly. Fold in the raisins.

Pour into pan. Mix topping with your fingers and sprinkle over top. Bake for 25 minutes. Cut into squares and serve warm.

Yield: 9 servings

# Lemon Raisin Coffee Cake

*This cake is quick and easy to make, with a lovely lemon flavor.*

1 cup all-purpose flour
½ cup whole wheat pastry flour
2½ teaspoons baking powder
¼ teaspoon salt
½ cup oat flour
½ cup raisins
1 tablespoon grated lemon rind
1 egg
¼ cup vegetable oil
¼ cup light honey
¾ cup skim milk
½ recipe Lemon Yogurt Glaze (page 139)
¼ cup finely chopped walnuts or pecans

Preheat the oven to 375° F. Grease a 9-inch square pan.

Sift together the all-purpose and whole wheat flours, baking powder, and salt into a bowl. Stir in the oat flour, raisins, and lemon rind; mix lightly to combine.

With an electric mixer, beat the egg until frothy, then beat in the oil, honey, and milk. With a wooden spoon, stir in the flour mixture until well mixed.

Pour the batter into the prepared pan, and bake for 25 to 30 minutes. Briefly cool the cake in the pan on a wire rack. Prepare the glaze and spoon over the warm cake. Sprinkle with the nuts. Cut into squares and serve warm.

Yield: 9 servings

# Banana Crunch Coffee Cake

**◆◆◆◆◆◆◆◆◆◆◆◆◆◆◆◆◆◆◆◆◆◆◆◆◆◆◆◆◆**

### Crunch Topping
¾ cup rolled oats
¼ cup firmly packed brown sugar
2 tablespoons melted margarine or
    vegetable oil
2 tablespoons finely chopped nuts
½ teaspoon cinnamon

### Cake
¼ cup vegetable oil
¼ cup brown sugar
¼ cup orange juice concentrate
¼ cup plain lowfat yogurt
1 cup mashed ripe bananas
2 eggs
1 teaspoon vanilla extract
1 cup oat flour
½ cup whole wheat pastry flour

¼ cup all purpose flour
1 teaspoon baking soda
¼ teaspoon salt
½ cup chopped nuts (optional)

Preheat the oven to 350° F. Grease an 8-inch square baking pan. Mix the topping ingredients and set aside.

Beat together the oil and brown sugar until light. Blend in the juice concentrate, yogurt, and bananas. Then beat in the eggs, one at a time, and the vanilla. Combine the dry ingredients and add them gradually. Stir in the nuts.

Pour into pan and sprinkle with the topping. Bake for 40 to 45 minutes. Cut into squares. Serve warm.

Yield: 9 servings

# Yogurt Pineapple Coffee Cake

### Cake
**1 cup whole wheat pastry flour**
**¼ cup oat flour**
**¼ cup wheat germ**
**2 teaspoons baking powder**
**¼ teaspoon salt**
**1 cup plain lowfat yogurt**
**½ cup crushed unsweetened pineapple, drained**
**¼ cup vegetable oil**
**½ cup raisins (optional)**

### Topping
**1 cup dried flaked coconut**
**⅓ cup light brown sugar**
**1 teaspoon cinnamon**

Preheat the oven to 350° F. Grease a 9-inch square pan or a 7-inch by 11-inch rectangular pan.

In a large bowl, combine the cake ingredients, except the raisins. Beat for 3 minutes at medium speed; stir in the raisins.

Pour the batter into the prepared pan. Combine the topping ingredients and sprinkle over the top. Bake for 35 to 40 minutes. Cool before cutting into squares. Serve warm or at room temperature.

Yield: 9 to 12 servings

### Variation
**Yogurt Pear Coffee Cake.** Use Crunch Topping (page 106) and substitute ½ cup pureed fresh unpeeled pears for the pineapple and nutmeg for the cinnamon.

# Maple Oat Bran Coffee Cake

1 cup oat bran
½ cup whole wheat pastry flour
2 tablespoons brown sugar, divided
1 tablespoon baking powder
1 teaspoon cinnamon
½ teaspoon nutmeg
1 egg white
1 egg
¼ cup vegetable oil
½ cup skim milk
¼ cup pure maple syrup
2 teaspoons vanilla extract
1½ cups chopped walnuts (optional)
2 tablespoons wheat germ

Preheat the oven to 375° F. Oil an 8-inch round cake pan.

Combine the oat bran, flour, 1 tablespoon of the brown sugar, the baking powder, and spices; stir well.

Beat the egg white until stiff and set aside. With the same beaters, beat together the egg, oil, milk, syrup, and vanilla. Stir in the dry ingredients, until just moistened. Add walnuts if you like. Gently fold in the egg white.

Spoon the batter into the prepared pan. Combine the remaining tablespoon of brown sugar with the wheat germ and sprinkle over the top. Bake for 30 minutes. Cool slightly. Cut into wedges and serve warm.

Yield: 6 to 8 servings

# 7
# *Tea Cakes and Loaf Cakes*

‹•‹•‹•‹•‹•‹•‹•‹•‹•‹•‹•‹•‹•‹•‹•‹•‹•‹•‹•‹•‹•‹•‹•‹•‹•‹•‹•‹•‹•‹•‹•‹•‹•‹•‹•‹•‹•‹•‹•‹•‹•

Afternoon tea is such a civilized institution and, to my mind, is a perfect way to entertain. In the best arrangement, people can sit down and really talk, partaking all the while of some lovely cakes.

The tea cake is a different species than the coffee cake. Usually eaten with the fingers, it's really the kind of thing that balances well on the tea saucer. It generally is not gooey, nor sticky. It tends to be dry and well behaved, staying neatly in one piece.

The loaf cake, often sliced and served with tea, is a quick bread strictly speaking, made in a loaf pan. It is generally sweeter than a bread, however. It makes good little tea sandwiches, and the ideal gift for your hostess or new neighbor. I like to bake loaf cakes in small pans (3 $\frac{5}{8}$ by 7 $\frac{3}{8}$ inches), wrap them in clear wrap, tie with bright ribbon or yarn, and present them as holiday gifts. They keep well, freeze well, and are easily sliced for the unexpected guests for breakfast, brunch, lunch, dinner, or—best of all—afternoon tea.

Several snacking cakes given in the first chapter work very well as loaf cakes. The baking time will be slightly more for the loaf pans.

These cakes are rich in whole grains, fruits, and nuts, while being low in fat and sugar. Very few need a topping or glaze. All are easily made.

# Orange Kiss-Me Cake

## Cake

1 cup whole wheat flour
3/4 cup all-purpose flour
1/4 cup wheat germ
2 tablespoons nonfat dry milk powder
1 teaspoon baking soda
1/4 teaspoon salt
1 (6-ounce) can orange juice concentrate, divided
1/4 cup vegetable oil
1/2 cup honey
2/3 cup skim milk
2 eggs
1 cup raisins
1/3 cup chopped walnuts

## Topping

1/4 cup sugar
1/4 cup chopped walnuts
1 teaspoon cinnamon

Preheat the oven to 350° F. Grease and flour a 9-inch by 13-inch pan.

Combine the dry ingredients and set aside. Measure 1/2 cup of the juice concentrate and mix it with the oil, honey, and milk until blended. Beat in the eggs, one at a time. Stir in the dry ingredients, then the raisins and nuts.

Bake for 40 to 45 minutes.

Drizzle the remaining juice concentrate over the top of the warm cake. Combine the topping ingredients and mix well. Sprinkle over the cake. Cool thoroughly before cutting.

Yield: 12 to 15 servings

# Peanut Butter Tea Cake

1 cup whole wheat pastry flour
1 cup all-purpose flour
2½ teaspoons baking powder
¼ teaspoon salt
½ cup oat flour
½ cup wheat germ
½ cup chunky peanut butter
¼ cup vegetable oil (peanut oil is fine)
⅓ cup honey
4 eggs
½ cup apple or white grape juice
     concentrate
3 tablespoons nonfat dry milk powder
1½ cups raisins

Preheat the oven to 325° F. Grease a 10-inch tube pan. Sift together the flours, baking powder, and salt. Stir in the oat flour and wheat germ. Set aside.

Cream the peanut butter and oil at high speed until blended; add the honey slowly and beat until smooth. Beat in the eggs, one at a time. Measure the concentrate and stir in the dry milk. Add to the creamed mixture alternately with flour mixture. Blend until smooth. Fold in the raisins.

Bake for 1 hour and 20 minutes. Cool for 10 minutes; remove from the pan and cool completely.

Yield: 8 to 10 servings

# Plum Cake

This recipe is a variation of a traditional German cake. It is customarily served with afternoon tea, accompanied by a large dollop of Schlag, that is, stiffly whipped unsweetened cream. We can all skip that, as the cake is quite wonderful by itself. Use Italian prune plums, if you possibly can.

½ cup whole wheat pastry flour
¼ cup all-purpose flour
1 tablespoon sugar
2 teaspoons baking powder
¼ teaspoon salt
¼ cup wheat germ
1½ tablespoons butter
1 egg

½ teaspoon vanilla extract
1 tablespoon apple or white grape juice
   concentrate
Approximately ½ tablespoon skim milk
Approximately 2 pounds plums, sliced or
   quartered
Sugar for topping
Light Whipped Topping (page 138)
   (optional)

Preheat the oven to 425° F. Grease a 10-inch pie plate or 8-inch square baking dish.

Sift together the flours, sugar, baking powder, and salt into a mixing bowl (or, if you like, blend the dough in a food processor). Stir in the wheat germ. Cut in the butter, then beat in the egg, vanilla, and juice concentrate. Add enough milk for the dough to hold together.

With floured hands, press the dough evenly on the bottom and sides of the prepared dish. Cover the top very closely with the plums, skin side down. Sprinkle with sugar. Bake for about 20 minutes. Serve cool.

Yield: 8 to 10 servings

## Variations

**German Apple Cake.** Instead of plums, cover the cake with unpeeled, thin apple wedges. Cortlands or early McIntosh apples work well. Sprinkle the top with cinnamon and sugar.

**German Peach Cake.** Instead of plums, cover the cake with peeled fresh or canned peach wedges and sprinkle the top with a mixture of nutmeg and sugar.

# Molasses Raisin Tea Loaf

*This moist and dark loaf combines the benefits of bran and molasses. It is very quickly made.*

1 cup whole wheat pastry flour
1 teaspoon baking soda
¼ teaspoon salt
1 egg
1 cup Kellogg's All-Bran cereal
½ cup raisins
2 tablespoons vegetable oil
¼ cup dark molasses
2 tablespoons apple juice concentrate
2 tablespoons nonfat dry milk powder
¼ cup very hot water

Preheat the oven to 350° F. Grease two small 3 ⅝-inch by 7 ⅜-inch loaf pans or one 5-inch by 9-inch pan.

Sift together the flour, baking soda, and salt. Set aside.

Beat the egg until foamy. Blend in the cereal, raisins, oil, and molasses. Add the juice concentrate and dry milk powder and stir well. Add the hot water and blend thoroughly. Stir in the dry ingredients, mixing only until combined.

Pour the batter into the prepared pan(s). Bake the small loaves for 35 minutes, the large loaf for 45 minutes. Cool for a few minutes and remove from the pan(s). Slice and serve while still warm.

Yield: 8 to 12 servings

114

# Fruit and Honey Tea Loaf

*Here is another tea loaf made with All-Bran cereal, this one with mixed dried fruit. Add ⅓ cup chopped walnuts, if you like.*

1½ cups Kellogg's All-Bran cereal
2 tablespoons light honey
¼ cup orange juice concentrate
½ cup finely cut apricots
¼ cup finely cut raisins
¼ cup finely cut pitted dates
1¼ cups boiling water
1 cup whole wheat pastry flour
½ cup oat flour or all-purpose flour
2 tablespoons nonfat dry milk powder
1 tablespoon baking powder
½ teaspoon salt
2 eggs
¼ cup vegetable oil

Measure the cereal, honey, juice concentrate, and dried fruit into a large mixing bowl. Pour the boiling water over, stir well, and let stand until most of the moisture is absorbed.

Preheat the oven to 350° F. Grease one 5-inch by 9-inch loaf pan or three 3 ⅝-inch by 7 ⅜-inch loaf pans.

Combine the dry ingredients and set aside.

Beat the eggs until light and add with the oil to the cereal and fruit mixture. Add the dry ingredients, stirring only until combined.

Spread the batter in the prepared pan(s) and bake the large pan for 55 minutes, the small pans for 45 to 50 minutes. Cool for a few minutes and remove from the pan(s). Cool thoroughly before slicing.

Yield: 8 to 12 servings

# Marmalade Tea Loaf

*I have always liked this tea bread because it contains no shortening.*

2 cups whole wheat pastry flour
½ cup all-purpose flour
2 teaspoons baking powder
1 teaspoon baking soda
½ teaspoon salt
½ cup oat flour
2 eggs
1½ cups low sugar orange marmalade
2 tablespoons honey
1 cup plain lowfat yogurt
1 tablespoon grated orange rind
½ cup unblanched slivered almonds, toasted
1 cup chopped cranberries

Preheat the oven to 350° F. Grease well one 5-inch by 9-inch loaf pan or three 3 ⅝-inch by 7 ⅜-inch pans.

Sift together the whole wheat and all-purpose flours, baking powder, baking soda, and salt into a large bowl. Stir in the oat flour.

Beat the eggs well and blend in the remaining ingredients. Fold this mixture into the dry ingredients; mix until just blended and no dry flour appears.

Pour the batter into the prepared pan(s). Bake the large loaf for about 1 hour, the smaller loaves for 45 to 50 minutes. Let cool for 5 to 10 minutes before removing from pan(s). Cool thoroughly before slicing.

Yield: 8 to 12 servings

# Banana Nut Loaf

*There are many recipes for banana breads, most of which contain much too much sugar and shortening. This one has no shortening at all. For an interesting flavor variation, try coarsely chopped roasted peanuts for the nuts.*

2 eggs
1/3 cup honey
3 large ripe bananas, mashed
1 cup whole wheat pastry flour
1/2 cup all-purpose flour
1 teaspoon baking soda
1/2 teaspoon salt
1/2 cup rolled oats or wheat germ
1/2 cup unblanched almonds or walnuts,
   coarsely chopped

Preheat the oven to 350° F. Grease a 5-inch by 9-inch loaf pan or two 3⅝-inch by 7⅜-inch loaf pans.

With an electric mixer, beat the eggs until light. Slowly beat in the honey; then add the bananas and mix thoroughly.

Sift together the whole wheat and all-purpose flours, baking soda, and salt; stir in the oats. Add this to the banana mixture and beat well. Stir in the nuts.

Pour the batter into the prepared pan(s) and bake the large pan for 1 hour, the smaller pans for 45 to 50 minutes. Cool for 10 minutes or so, then remove from the pan(s). Cool completely before slicing.

Yield: 8 to 10 servings

# Cranberry Orange Tea Bread

1 cup all-purpose flour
½ cup oat flour
¼ cup whole wheat pastry flour
¼ cup soy flour
¼ cup sugar
1½ teaspoons baking powder
½ teaspoon baking soda
¼ teaspoon salt
1 orange
Orange juice concentrate
2 tablespoons vegetable oil
1 egg, well beaten
1 cup chopped walnuts
2 cups cranberries, cut in half or
    coarsely chopped

Preheat the oven to 350° F. Grease a 5-inch by 9-inch loaf pan.

Mix the dry ingredients. Set aside.

Remove the seeds and some of the pulp from the orange, then grind it in a food grinder. Combine it with the oil and orange juice concentrate to make ¾ cup. Stir in the beaten egg. Pour this mixture into the dry ingredients. Stir to mix well; add the nuts and cranberries.

Spoon into the pan. Run a groove down the middle of the loaf with the back of a spoon. Bake the loaf for 60 minutes. This cake will slice more easily the next day.

Yield: 8 to 10 servings

# Glazed Lemon-Nut Bread

**Bread**
2 tablespoons butter, softened
1 tablespoon margarine, softened
2 tablespoons sugar
¼ cup honey
2 eggs
1 tablespoon grated lemon rind
1 cup all-purpose flour
2½ teaspoons baking powder
½ teaspoon salt
½ cup wheat germ
½ cup oat flour
½ cup orange juice concentrate
⅓ cup skim milk
2 tablespoons nonfat dry milk powder
½ cup chopped walnuts

**Glaze**
2 tablespoons sugar
1 tablespoon lemon juice

Preheat the oven to 350° F. Grease a 5-inch by 9-inch loaf pan. Cream the butter and margarine with the sugar and honey until light . Add the eggs and lemon rind and beat well. Sift together the flour, baking powder, and salt. Stir in the wheat germ and oat flour.

Combine the juice concentrate, milk, and dry milk. Add to the creamed mixture alternately with the dry ingredients. Stir in the walnuts. Bake for 50 to 55 minutes. Let cool for 10 minutes. Prepare the glaze and spoon over the warm bread.

Yield: 8 to 10 servings

# *Pear Loaf*

2 tablespoons butter, softened
2 tablespoons margarine, softened
¼ cup sugar
2 eggs
1 cup all-purpose flour
½ cup whole wheat pastry flour
½ cup oat flour
1 teaspoon baking powder
½ teaspoon baking soda
½ teaspoon salt
½ teaspoon nutmeg
¼ cup plain lowfat yogurt or buttermilk
¼ cup apple or white grape juice
    concentrate
1 cup chopped pears, unpeeled
1 teaspoon vanilla extract

Preheat the oven to 350° F. Grease a 5-inch by 9-inch loaf pan.

Cream the butter and margarine and gradually beat in the sugar. Beat in the eggs, one at a time.

Combine the dry ingredients. Mix together the yogurt and juice concentrate and add to the egg mixture alternately with the dry ingredients. Stir in the pears and vanilla.

Pour the batter into the prepared pan and bake for 1 hour. Cool for about 10 minutes before removing from the pan. Cool thoroughly before slicing.

Yield: 8 to 10 servings

# Pineapple Pecan Loaf

*This loaf combines crushed pineapple, orange juice concentrate, and whole grains. It should be sliced very thin.*

3 tablespoons margarine
½ cup light brown sugar
1 egg
1 cup all-purpose flour
¾ cup whole wheat pastry flour
1 teaspoon baking soda
¼ teaspoon salt
½ cup wheat germ
2 tablespoons nonfat dry milk powder
1 (6-ounce) can orange juice concentrate
1 (8-ounce) can crushed unsweetened
  pineapple, with juice
½ cup chopped pecans

Preheat the oven to 350° F. Grease one 5-inch by 9-inch loaf pan or two 3⅝-inch by 7⅜-inch loaf pans.

Cream the margarine with the sugar. Add the egg and beat very well.

Sift together the flours, baking soda, and salt. Mix in the wheat germ and dry milk powder. Add to the creamed mixture alternately with the juice concentrate. Then stir in the pineapple and nuts.

Pour the batter into the prepared pan(s). Bake the large loaf for 1 hour, the smaller loaves for about 50 minutes. Cool for about 10 minutes and remove from the pan(s). Cool thoroughly before slicing.

Yield: 10 to 12 servings

# Raisin Tea Loaf

*Here is a typical British raisin cake for afternoon tea.*

2 cups raisins
¼ cup honey
½ cup orange, white grape, or apple juice
  concentrate
¼ cup hot water
3 tablespoons butter
1 cup whole wheat pastry flour
¾ cup all-purpose flour
¼ cup wheat germ
2 teaspoons baking powder
¼ teaspoon salt
1 large egg, well beaten

In a saucepan, combine the raisins, honey, juice concentrate, and hot water. Boil for 2 minutes. Stir in the butter and cool.

Preheat the oven to 350° F. Grease and flour a 5-inch by 9-inch loaf pan.

Mix together the dry ingredients and stir in the cooled raisin mixture. Then fold in the beaten egg.

Spoon the batter into the prepared pan and bake for 1 to 1¼ hours. Cool in the pan for 10 minutes, then remove. The cake may be served warm or cooled.

Yield: 8 to 10 servings

### Variation

**Currant Tea Loaf.** Substitute 2 cups dried currants for the raisins. Use apple or white grape juice concentrate.

# Chunky Apple Walnut Loaf

*A tasty apple and nut combination, this quickly prepared loaf is sweetened with honey and has a simple authenticity about it. You can see the chunks of apples and nuts.*

⅓ **cup vegetable oil**
½ **cup apple juice concentrate**
¼ **cup honey**
**2 large eggs**
**1 teaspoon vanilla extract**
¼ **cup plain lowfat yogurt**
**2 tablespoons nonfat dry milk powder**
**1 teaspoon baking soda**
¼ **teaspoon salt**
1½ **cups whole wheat pastry flour**
½ **cup wheat germ**
**1 cup walnuts, coarsely chopped**

**1 medium-size tart apple, coarsely chopped (do not peel)**

Grease two 3 ⅝-inch by 7 ⅜-inch loaf pans.

In a large bowl, mix the oil, juice concentrate, honey, eggs, vanilla, and yogurt. Beat well. Then stir in the dry milk powder, baking soda, and salt, mixing well. Combine the flour with the wheat germ and mix in with the nuts and apple. Stir everything into the batter.

Pour the batter into the prepared pans. Place them in a cold oven, set it for 350° F., and bake for about 50 minutes. Cool for 10 minutes and remove from the pans. Cool thoroughly before slicing.

Yield: 10 servings

# *Honey Cake*

1 cup honey
1½ cups all-purpose flour
1 cup whole wheat pastry flour
1 cup skim milk or buttermilk
2 tablespoons wheat germ
1½ teaspoons baking powder
1 teaspoon baking soda
½ teaspoon anise seed
⅛ teaspoon ground cloves

Preheat the oven to 350° F. Grease a 5-inch by 9-inch loaf pan.

Put the honey in a mixing bowl. Alternately add a little flour and a little milk. Beat well until smooth. Continue slowly adding flour and milk, a little at a time, beating all the while. Then stir in the remaining ingredients. The batter will be very sticky and thick.

Spoon the batter into the prepared pan and bake for a little over an hour, sometimes a little longer. Baking time really depends on the honey. The cake is done when it begins to pull away from the side of the pan and a cake tester, inserted in the center of the loaf, comes out clean. You can also bake this cake in two smaller loaves; baking time will be about 50 minutes.

Cool for about 10 minutes before removing from the pan. Make sure this cake is completely cool before you slice it. It can be cut in very thin slices.

Yield: 10 to 12 servings

# 8
# *Fruitcakes*

❖◀❖◀❖◀❖◀❖◀❖◀❖◀❖◀❖◀❖◀❖◀❖◀❖◀❖◀❖◀❖◀❖◀❖◀❖◀❖◀❖◀❖◀❖◀❖◀❖◀❖◀❖◀❖◀❖◀❖◀❖◀❖◀❖▶

Fruitcakes are an established part of our holiday tradition. Different than cakes with fruit, they are notable for being rich, compact, and chock full of dried fruits and nuts. Often they are laced with sherry or rum or brandy, and unlike most other cakes, they definitely improve with age.

Also unlike other cakes, fruitcakes do not enjoy universal popularity. One friend claims that the fruitcake his aunt sends him for Christmas every year gets used as a doorstop. Personally, I find that fruitcake seems to be always there when you need a little something to go with a beverage or a fruit compote. And it does wear very well. We had a light fruitcake for our wedding and on our first anniversary we ate a piece that had been in the freezer for almost a year. It was as good as the day it was baked! What other cake can give you such thin slices? And what could be better on a cold evening with a cup of tea or a glass of white wine or a touch of rum punch?

The nutritional benefits of fruits and nuts have been discussed earlier. And here are cakes fairly bursting with them. Although fruitcakes are known for being rich, the cakes here call for less butter and sugar than traditional fruitcakes and are rich in the fiber and nutrients of whole grains, fruits, and fruit juices. Try to avoid using too many commercial candied fruits, as they are glacéed in heavy sugar syrup and contain additives. Any supermarket can supply you with dried raisins, apricots, dates, and currants. Other dried fruits are easily obtained at health food stores or at stores that sell in bulk.

There are two easy ways to chop dried fruit, neither requiring a food chopper. Cutting the fruit with a very sharp knife on a wooden board is quick and simple. Kitchen scissors, dipped frequently in cold water, also work well.

# Fruity Fruitcake

1 cup walnut halves
1 cup pecan halves
1 cup Brazil nuts
2 cups pitted dates
2 cups dried apricots
12 pitted prunes, cut in quarters
$\frac{1}{2}$ cup dried currants
$\frac{1}{2}$ cup raisins
1 cup whole wheat pastry flour
$\frac{1}{2}$ cup all-purpose flour
1 teaspoon baking powder
$\frac{1}{2}$ teaspoon salt
6 eggs
$\frac{1}{2}$ cup sugar
2 teaspoons vanilla extract
4 tablespoons brandy, divided

Grease a 5-inch by 9-inch loaf pan. Line with brown paper and grease the paper. Combine the nuts and fruits in a large bowl. Sift the flours, baking powder, and salt over them and toss lightly until well coated.

Preheat the oven to 275° F. Beat the eggs, sugar, and vanilla with an electric mixer until fluffy and light. Pour over the nut mixture and stir gently to combine. Fill the pan, pressing the mixture firmly. Bake for 2 hours. Remove the pan to a rack and spoon 2 tablespoons of brandy over the cake. Let stand for 1 hour. Then invert the cake, remove the pan, and peel off the paper. Turn the cake right side up and cool completely. Place on a plate and spoon the remaining 2 tablespoons brandy over the top. To store, wrap the cake in cheesecloth that has been soaked in brandy. Wrap in heavy foil.

Yield: 12 servings

# Golden Fruitcake

2 cups quartered dried apricots
1 cup pitted dates, coarsely chopped
1 cup golden raisins
1 tablespoon grated orange rind
¾ cup orange juice concentrate
½ cup all-purpose flour
½ teaspoon baking powder
Dash of salt
½ cup oat flour
⅓ cup skim milk
3 eggs, well beaten
1 teaspoon vanilla extract
1 cup coarsely chopped almonds
1 cup coarsely chopped walnuts

Grease a 5-inch by 9-inch loaf pan. Line the bottom and sides of the pan with waxed paper. Grease the paper. In a mixing bowl, combine the dried fruits and orange rind. Heat the juice concentrate to boiling and pour over the fruit, stirring well; set aside.

Preheat the oven to 300° F. Sift the flour, baking powder, and salt. Stir in the oat flour. Set aside.

Measure the milk into a large cup, beat in the eggs and vanilla. Stir this into the fruit mixture alternately with the dry ingredients. Stir in nuts.

Bake for 1½ hours. Cool thoroughly, remove from the pan, and take off the paper. Wrap tightly. Chill for several days before slicing.

Yield: 10 to 12 servings

# *Applesauce Fruitcake*

*This simple fruitcake is economical and lighter in texture than the usual fruitcake.*

¼ cup margarine
½ cup light molasses or dark honey
¼ cup apple juice concentrate
¾ cup slightly sweetened applesauce
Grated rind and juice of 1 orange
1 tablespoon rum or brandy
2 eggs
1 cup whole wheat pastry flour
1 cup all-purpose flour
¼ cup oat flour
¼ cup wheat germ
1 teaspoon baking powder
1 teaspoon baking soda
¼ teaspoon salt
1½ teaspoons cinnamon
½ teaspoon nutmeg
½ teaspoon cloves
½ teaspoon ginger
1 cup golden raisins
1 cup mixed diced fruit (apricots, dates, currants)
1 cup chopped walnuts
Additional walnut halves for garnish (optional)

Preheat the oven to 325° F. Grease a 9-inch tube pan; line the bottom with waxed paper.

Cream the margarine with the molasses until fluffy. Beat in the juice concentrate, applesauce, orange rind and juice, rum, and eggs.

Measure the dry ingredients and reserve ½ cup flour for the fruit. Toss the dry ingredients to mix well. Add to the liquid mixture and blend well. Combine the fruits and nuts and toss with the reserved flour. Fold into the batter.

Pour the batter into the prepared pan and garnish with walnut halves, if desired. Bake for 1¼ hours, or until a tester inserted into the center of the cake comes out clean. Let stand for 20 minutes in the pan. Remove from the pan and cool completely. Store in a cool place.

Yield: 10 to 12 servings

# *Banana Fruitcake*

❥❥❥❥❥❥❥❥❥❥❥❥❥❥❥❥❥❥❥❥❥❥❥❥❥❥❥❥❥❥❥❥❥❥❥

### *Cake*

**1 cup whole wheat pastry flour**
**½ cup all-purpose flour**
**1½ teaspoons baking powder**
**½ teaspoon salt**
**2 cups large pecan halves or whole Brazil**
    **nuts (do not chop)**
**2 cups coarsely chopped pitted dates**
**1 cup golden raisins or dried currants**
**3 cups sliced ripe bananas**
    **(3 to 4 bananas)**
**4 eggs**
**¼ cup sugar**

### *Glaze*

**¼ cup orange juice concentrate**
**¼ cup water**
**2 tablespoons light honey**

Preheat the oven to 300° F. Grease a 5-inch by 9-inch loaf pan. Line with waxed paper and grease the paper. Sift the flours, baking powder, and salt into a bowl. Add the nuts and dried fruit and stir. Mash the bananas in another bowl. Add the eggs and sugar and beat until fluffy. Fold into the flour mixture.

Bake for 2 hours. Cool in the pan on a rack for 15 minutes.

Remove the cake from the pan, and pull off the paper and cool. Boil the glaze ingredients for 2 minutes. Spoon the hot glaze over the cake. Wrap well and store in a cool place.

Yield: 10 to 12 servings

# Mincemeat Fruitcake

2 cups prepared Nonesuch® mincemeat
2 cups diced dried fruit (prunes, apricots,
   raisins, dates, currants)
1 cup chopped walnuts
1 cup whole wheat pastry flour
1 cup all-purpose flour
½ cup wheat germ
½ teaspoon baking powder
½ teaspoon baking soda
¼ teaspoon salt
2 tablespoons butter, softened
2 tablespoons margarine, softened
½ cup dark brown sugar
1 teaspoon vanilla extract
2 eggs
Brandy Glaze (page 139)

Preheat the oven to 325° F. Grease a 10-inch fluted tube pan. Combine the mincemeat, fruits, and nuts in a bowl. Stir together the dry ingredients and mix them in.

Cream the butter, margarine, brown sugar, and vanilla. Beat in the eggs. Fold in the dry ingredients and fruit and nuts.

Bake for 65 minutes. Cool for 10 minutes. Remove from pan. Drizzle the glaze over the warm cake. When completely cool, wrap in a cheesecloth soaked in brandy. Wrap again in foil. Store for at least a week before cutting.

Yield: 10 to 12 servings

# No-Flour Fruit and Spice Cake

❖➤❖➤❖➤❖➤❖➤❖➤❖➤❖➤❖➤❖➤❖➤❖➤❖➤❖➤❖➤❖➤❖➤❖➤❖➤❖➤❖➤❖➤❖➤❖➤❖➤❖➤

¾ cup apple juice or cider, boiling
½ cup pitted prunes, chopped
¾ cup raisins and/or currants
1 cup pitted dates, chopped
2 tablespoons vegetable oil
¼ cup potato starch or cornstarch
1 teaspoon baking powder
½ teaspoon baking soda
¼ teaspoon salt
1½ teaspoons cinnamon
½ teaspoon nutmeg
¼ teaspoon cloves
¼ teaspoon allspice
1 cup packed finely ground walnuts
1 cup packed finely ground hazelnuts
5 eggs, separated

Grease and flour an 8-inch round pan. Pour the apple juice over the prunes and raisins. Mash the dates with the oil. Sift the potato starch with the baking powder, baking soda, salt, and spices. Combine with the ground nuts.

Preheat the oven to 275° F. Beat the egg yolks, one at a time, into the date-oil mixture. Blend in the nut mixture and then the dried fruit mixture.

Beat the egg whites until stiff but not dry. Fold half into the batter, blending well. Fold in the second half, very gently.

Bake for 2 hours. Cool for 15 minutes, then remove from the pan. When completely cool, wrap tightly in plastic wrap and store in a cool place.

Yield: 8 to 10 servings

# 9
# *Frostings, Glazes, Toppings, & Fillings*

◆◆◆◆◆◆◆◆◆◆◆◆◆◆◆◆◆◆◆◆◆◆◆◆◆◆◆◆◆◆◆◆◆◆◆◆◆◆◆◆◆◆◆◆◆◆◆

There are many different possibilities for covering, filling, or accompanying your cake. Some are even possibilities for beautification. As a general rule, a good cake needs very little added to it, and too often the customary additions are laden with hidden and empty calories. Here are some suggestions for light accompaniments. Use fresh fruit whenever you possibly can, and be sure to use freshly squeezed lemon juice and freshly grated lemon rind. Remember that the taste for something sweet is only relative and easily scaled down.

In most cases I have indicated a specific accompaniment for a cake and the recipe for it appears here. But some recipes in this chapter have not been mentioned before and appear here simply as additions to the repertory. Also, different people have different tastes and ideas for what goes with their cakes. Some people like a firm fruit topping for cheesecake, whereas others prefer a saucelike covering. Here is the chance to exercise your personal preferences, or to try something totally new.

Several recipes for toppings that are baked right on the cake appear elsewhere, especially in the chapter on coffee cakes. They are also useful. A listing appears in the index under toppings.

## Fluffy Frosting

To my taste, this classic frosting is the only choice for a chocolate layer cake. As it contains no butter or egg yolks, it is a good choice for the cholesterol watcher. It is easily made and truly foolproof. The recipe makes a generous amount for the tops and sides of two 9-inch layers. Cut it in half for a smaller cake.

Measure 2 cups powdered sugar into a small saucepan and stir in 6 tablespoons hot water. Cover and boil until the sugar is dissolved, only a minute or so.

Combine 2 egg whites, ½ teaspoon cream of tartar, and ⅛ teaspoon salt in a mixing bowl and beat slightly. Slowly add the hot sugar syrup, beating all the time. Set the mixer to medium-high speed and beat for 2 minutes, then to high speed for 2 to 3 minutes more, or until the frosting is the right consistency to spread. Add 1 teaspoon vanilla extract while beating.

To make Honey Fluffy Frosting, substitute 1 cup light honey for the powdered sugar and water in the recipe. Heat the honey to boiling and beat it in slowly as above.

To make Orange Fluffy Frosting, use 1¾ cups powdered sugar. Substitute 3 tablespoons orange juice concentrate for 3 tablespoons water. Proceed as above, beating in 2 teaspoons grated orange rind with the vanilla.

## Light Butter Frosting

Combine 1½ cups powdered sugar, 1 tablespoon soft butter, ½ teaspoon vanilla extract, dash of salt, and 2 tablespoons milk. Beat until smooth. If the frosting is too thick, add a little more milk. If too thin, add a little more sugar. This makes enough for drizzling over the top and sizes of an 8-inch layer cake or a 9-inch or 10-inch tube cake.

## Maple Butter Icing

Cream 2 tablespoons soft sweet butter with 1 cup pure maple sugar until smooth. Blend in 1 teaspoon vanilla extract and about 2 tablespoons water, enough to make the icing easy to spread. Enough for a single-layer 8-inch cake.

## Lemon Milk Icing

In a blender, whirl ½ cup honey and the grated rind of 1 medium-size lemon. Add ¾ cup dry milk powder and blend for a minute, or until very smooth. Allow to stand for 30 minutes or so before using. This is enough for a light spread over an 8-inch or 9-inch square cake.

## Easy Chocolate Frosting

Cream 1 tablespoon softened margarine with ¾ cup powdered sugar until smooth. Add 2 tablespoons unsweetened baking cocoa, 2 tablespoons skim milk, and ½ teaspoon vanilla extract. Beat until very smooth. This makes a thin layer for a small cake. You can double or triple it for a larger cake.

## Creamy Cheese Topping

The traditional frosting for carrot cake, this topping has many other uses as well. The amount is adequate for a square or rectangular sheet cake.

Combine 8 ounces lowfat cream cheese or farmer cheese, at room temperature, with 1 tablespoon grated lemon rind, 2 tablespoons orange juice concentrate, and ½ teaspoon vanilla extract. Beat until fluffy. Keep refrigerated.

To make Honey Cream Cheese Topping, substitute 2 tablespoons honey for the orange juice concentrate.

Make Cottage Cheese Creamy Topping in a blender or food processor. Substitute 1 cup lowfat cottage cheese, well drained, for the cream cheese. Use 1 tablespoon orange juice concentrate, or enough to make a spreadable consistency.

Make Ricotta Cream Topping in a food processor. Substitute 1 cup part skim or lite ricotta for the cream cheese. Add 2 tablespoons plain lowfat yogurt and $^1/2$ teaspoon cinnamon. If you like, substitute 2 tablespoons light honey for the juice concentrate. This makes about $1^1/$ 4 cups.

To make Ricotta Cream Filling, add 1 tablespoon powdered sugar. Stir in 2 tablespoons finely chopped nuts, if desired.

## Chestnut Crème

Chestnuts are good food, with the benefits of nuts and fewer calories—well worth the effort to prepare them. Take 2 pounds fresh chestnuts and remove the shells. The easiest way to do this is to score them and bake them in a moderate oven for about 20 minutes; then peel them. Next, steam the chestnuts in a little water until soft. Remove the inner skins. Place the chestnuts in a blender or food processor and puree until smooth. Heat $^1/2$ cup honey to boiling with $^1/4$ cup apple juice concentrate and add to the chestnuts; blend until smooth. Then add 1 teaspoon vanilla extract and 2 tablespoons nonfat dry milk powder. Blend until very, very smooth. Thin, if necessary, with a little skim milk. This makes a delicious filling or frosting for a chocolate cake. Makes about 3 cups.

## Light Whipped Topping

There is another version of this topping, made without gelatin. It is less stable. This one will keep, refrigerated, for several days.

Chill ½ cup evaporated skimmed milk (along with the beaters) in the freezer for about 30 minutes. In a small saucepan, sprinkle 1 package unflavored gelatin over ¼ cup unsweetened fruit juice. Heat slowly, stirring, until the gelatin dissolves. Pour into a mixer bowl, add 1 tablespoon sugar and ½ teaspoon vanilla extract. Chill thoroughly. Add the chilled milk and beat at very high speed until very thick. Keep refrigerated. Makes about 3 cups.

## Light Milk Topping

In a small mixing bowl, combine ½ cup nonfat dry milk powder, ¼ cup frozen fruit juice concentrate (apple or white grape juice are the best), ¼ cup water, 1 tablespoon lemon juice, and 1 teaspoon vanilla extract. Beat at high speed for about 10 minutes, or until stiff. Serve immediately. Makes about 1 cup.

## Easy Glaze

Blend ½ cup powdered sugar with 1 tablespoon lemon juice. Add enough water or fruit juice to thin to the desired consistency. This is sufficient to lightly cover a small cake or a loaf cake.

### Milk and Honey Glaze

Combine 1 cup powdered sugar with 2 tablespoons light honey and 1 tablespoon milk. Add more milk if needed to reach the desired consistency. This is sufficient to drizzle over the top of a small cake or a 9-inch or 10-inch tube cake.

### Brandy Glaze

Combine ¾ cup powdered sugar, 1 tablespoon brandy, ½ teaspoon vanilla extract. Add enough water to reach desired consistency. This makes enough to lightly cover the top of a small cake or loaf cake.

### Lemon Yogurt Glaze

Blend 1 cup powdered sugar with 2 tablespoons freshly squeezed lemon juice and 2 tablespoons plain lowfat yogurt. Stir until smooth. If too thick, add several more drops of lemon juice. Stir in 1 teaspoon grated lemon rind, if desired. This is sufficient for a 9-inch round or 8-inch square cake.

To make an Orange Yogurt Glaze, substitute fresh orange juice and rind for the lemon juice.

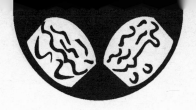

## Orange Glaze

Unlike the preceding glazes, this one is cooked. It makes a fine tangy topping for cheesecake. Combine ½ cup orange juice concentrate, ½ cup water, 2 tablespoons honey, 1 tablespoon lemon juice, and 1 tablespoon cornstarch in a small saucepan. Heat, stirring, to boiling and continue to cook until thick and clear. Cool before covering the cake. Makes about 1¼ cups.

## Apricot Glaze

Cover 1 cup chopped apricots in equal parts of apple juice concentrate and water. Heat to boiling, turn off the heat, and allow apricots to soak for several hours. Then simmer, uncovered, over low heat, stirring occasionally, until the apricots are very soft and the liquid is absorbed. Puree in a food processor until smooth. Return to the saucepan, add 1 tablespoon honey and 1 teaspoon cornstarch dissolved in 2 tablespoons water. Cook until thickened, about 3 minutes. Cool before spreading. Makes about 1⅓ cups.

## Blueberry Topping

This and the following cooked fruit toppings make a good accompaniment for angel food cake, sponge cake, cheesecake, or cottage pudding.

In a saucepan, mix together 3 tablespoons fruit juice concentrate (orange, orange pineapple, apple, or white grape), 1 tablespoon lemon juice, and 1 tablespoon water with 1 tablespoon cornstarch. Stir in 2 cups fresh blueberries (or frozen, thawed, with their juice). Cook, stirring, over medium heat until the mixture comes to a full boil. Simmer for 3 minutes. Remove from the heat. Cool before spooning over the top of cake. Makes about 2½ cups.

## Cherry Topping

Put 2 cups fresh pitted sour cherries in a bowl and sprinkle 2 tablespoons sugar and 3 tablespoons thawed apple or white grape juice concentrate over them. Stir well and let stand for 30 minutes. Drain off all the liquid into a saucepan. To the liquid, add 1 tablespoon lemon juice and 2 tablespoons cornstarch. Cook, stirring, until boiling. Reduce the heat and boil for 3 minutes, or until thickened and clear. Cool slightly, stir in the cherries and ¼ teaspoon almond extract. Cool before spooning over the cake. Makes about 2¼ cups.

To make Cherry Sauce, use only 1 tablespoon cornstarch and serve warm.

## Pineapple Apricot Topping

Place ³/₄ cup dried apricots in a small saucepan. Drain the juice from an 8-ounce can of unsweetened crushed pineapple into a large measuring cup. Set the pineapple aside for later.

Add additional fruit juice (pineapple, pineapple orange, or orange) to measure 1 cup. Pour this over the apricots and cook on low heat for about 30 minutes, or until the apricots are very tender. Puree the apricot mixture in a blender or food processor with 1 tablespoon honey and 1 tablespoon fruit juice concentrate (orange or pineapple orange). Return the mixture to the saucepan and stir in the reserved pineapple and 1 teaspoon grated orange rind. Cook over low heat, stirring constantly, for about 5 minutes, or until thickened. Makes about 1¹/₂ cups.

## Pineapple Orange Sauce

Combine 1 cup orange juice, ¹/₄ cup light honey, ¹/₄ cup crushed unsweetened pineapple with its juice, ¹/₄ cup raisins, and 1 apple, peeled and chopped, in a saucepan. Bring to a boil, slowly, stirring frequently; then reduce the heat and simmer 30 minutes, stirring from time to time. Serve warm over cake. Makes about 2 cups.

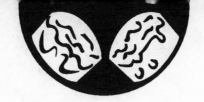

## Fresh Strawberry Sauce

Into a food processor with steel blade, measure 2 cups whole strawberries and ¼ cup sugar or 2 tablespoons light honey. Process until pureed. Then stir in 1 tablespoon lemon juice and 3 cups strawberries, cut in quarters. Wonderful for shortcake. Makes about 4 cups.

For a Cooked Strawberry Sauce, measure 2 cups fresh strawberries and process until smooth. Combine in saucepan with 2 tablespoons sugar, ½ teaspoon grated orange rind, 2 tablespoons orange juice concentrate, and 1 heaping tablespoon cornstarch. Cook, stirring, until thickened and clear. Cool thoroughly before serving. Makes about 1¼ cups.

## Fresh Currant Sauce

If your currant bushes are producing well, try making this extraordinary sauce to serve over cheesecake or sponge cake.

Measure 4 cups currants (use the largest and ripest you have). Sprinkle ½ cup sugar over them, stir well, and let stand for 30 minutes. Drain off the liquid into a saucepan and combine it with ½ cup apple juice concentrate, ⅓ cup water, and 2 tablespoons cornstarch. Cook, stirring, until the mixture boils and thickens. Add the currants and simmer for 3 minutes. Cool slightly before serving. Makes about 4½ cups.

For Fresh Currant and Raspberry Sauce, use 2 cups currants and 2 cups fresh ripe red raspberries. Reduce the sugar to ⅓ cup.

143

## Melba Sauce

Place 2 cups fresh red raspberries in a small saucepan with ¼ cup apple juice concentrate and 2 tablespoons water. Cook gently until the berries are very soft. Press the mixture through a sieve and return the strained juice to the saucepan. Blend in 2 teaspoons cornstarch and bring to a boil, stirring constantly, until thickened and clear. Stir in 2 tablespoons homemade currant jelly until completely melted. Serve cool. Makes about 1¼ cups.

## Rum Raisin Sauce

This sauce reminds me of cold winter nights. It is excellent over sponge cake or cottage pudding. It keeps for a long time in the refrigerator.

In a saucepan, combine 3 tablespoons honey, 3 tablespoons apple or white grape juice concentrate, 1 tablespoon butter, grated rind of 1 lemon, 1 cup golden raisins, 2 tablespoons lemon juice, and 1 cup water. Stir in 1 tablespoon cornstarch and a dash of salt. Bring to a boil, stirring, and simmer for 4 to 5 minutes. Cool slightly and add 2 tablespoons dark rum. Serve warm. Makes about 2 cups.

## Cider Sauce

A great sauce for gingerbread. Combine ¼ cup light honey, ¼ cup apple juice concentrate, 2 tablespoons cornstarch, 2 cups apple cider, and 2 tablespoons lemon juice in a saucepan. Bring to a boil, stirring; reduce the heat and simmer for 3 minutes. Cool slightly and blend in 1 tablespoon butter. Serve warm. Makes about 2½ cups.

## Hot Applesauce Topping

A very good topping for gingerbread or sponge cake, very quickly made. In a saucepan, combine 2 cups slightly sweetened applesauce, 1 teaspoon cinnamon, a dash of nutmeg, 2 tablespoons brown sugar, 2 tablespoons apple juice concentrate, and 1 teaspoon lemon juice. Heat until very warm and the sugar is dissolved. Makes about 2 cups.

## Pear Butter

Wash fresh pears; do not peel. Core and slice into a food processor. Process until smooth; continue until you have 2 cups of puree. Mix it with ¼ cup light honey, ¼ cup apple juice concentrate, 1 tablespoon lemon juice, ½ teaspoon cinnamon, and ½ teaspoon nutmeg. Cook slowly until thick, stirring frequently. Or bake in a rectangular pan at 300° F., stirring from time to time, until thickened to the desired consistency. Makes about 2 cups.

## Apple Butter

Follow the same procedure as for Pear Butter, using tart apples. It is not necessary to peel them. Increase the cinnamon to 1 teaspoon and add ½ teaspoon allspice as well.

## Cranberry-Orange Relish

Grind 4 cups raw cranberries in a food grinder, using a medium to coarse blade, and cook with ½ cup apple juice concentrate and ½ cup honey until thickened. Then grind 2 apples (core and seeds removed, but do not peel) and 1 orange (seeds and some pith removed) and stir them into the cooled cranberry mixture. Cool and store in the refrigerator. This topping will keep for weeks. Makes about 4 cups.

## Lemon Sauce

For many people, this is the only possible topping for cottage pudding and gingerbread.

Combine 2 tablespoons light honey, 2 tablespoons white grape juice concentrate, 1 tablespoon cornstarch, and a dash of salt in a small saucepan. Gradually stir in 1 cup boiling water. Cook, stirring constantly, for about 5 minutes, or until thickened and clear. Stir in 1 tablespoon butter, 1 teaspoon grated lemon rind, and 3 tablespoons lemon juice. Serve warm. Makes about 1½ cups.

## Orange Sauce

As this sauce is designed to accompany the Passover Cake, it is made with potato starch. Feel free to substitute cornstarch, and to use it over other cakes.

Combine 2 cups orange juice, ¼ cup light honey, and 2 tablespoons apple juice concentrate in a saucepan. Stir in 1 tablespoon cornstarch and cook, stirring, until thickened. Peel 2 oranges, remove the seeds and pith, and cut in sections. Add them to the sauce and reheat gently. Serve warm. Makes about 2½ cups.

## Carob Sauce

Here is a good substitute for those people who cannot or should not have chocolate. In a small saucepan, combine ½ cup carob powder with ¼ cup honey and ½ cup skim or 2% lowfat milk. Blend well and boil for several minutes. Stir in 1 teaspoon butter and 1 teaspoon vanilla extract. Makes about ¾ cup.

## Lemon Cake Filling

In a saucepan, mix 2 tablespoons cornstarch with ¼ cup apple juice concentrate, ¼ cup honey, ¼ cup water, and 3 tablespoons lemon juice until smooth. Cook over medium heat, stirring constantly, until thickened and clear. Remove from the heat, stir in 1 tablespoon butter and 1 teaspoon grated lemon peel. Cool thoroughly. Makes about 1¼ cups, sufficient to fill an 8-inch or 9-inch layer cake.

## Orange Cake Filling

Here is a good filling for cake rolls or layer cakes. Combine ½ cup orange juice concentrate, ½ cup water, 2½ tablespoons cornstarch, a dash of salt, and 2 tablespoons lemon juice in a saucepan. Cook, stirring, until boiling and thickened. Cook for 3 minutes more. Cool slightly, stir in 1 teaspoon grated orange rind and 1 tablespoon Grand Marnier, Cointreau, rum, or brandy. Cool thoroughly. Makes about 1⅓ cups.

## Creamy Filling

Another filling for cake rolls, this one has a cream cheese base. Blend 8 ounces lowfat cream cheese or farmer cheese, softened, with 2 tablespoons powdered sugar, 2 tablespoons orange juice concentrate, and ½ teaspoon vanilla until very smooth. Stir in 2 tablespoons finely chopped pecans. Makes about 1¼ cups.

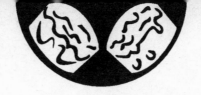

❖◗❖◗❖◗❖◗❖◗❖◗❖◗❖◗❖◗❖◗❖◗❖◗❖◗❖◗❖◗❖◗❖◗❖◗❖◗❖◗❖◗❖◗❖◗❖◗❖◗❖◗❖◗❖◗❖◗❖◗❖◗❖◗❖◗

## Peanut Butter Filling

This makes an ideal filling or topping for banana cakes. Combine 1 tablespoon dry milk powder, a dash of nutmeg, 2 tablespoons apple juice concentrate, 1 tablespoon honey, and ½ cup crunchy peanut butter. Blend very well. If too thick, add just a little apple juice. Makes about ¾ cup.

## Custard Filling

This recipe comes from my mother, who made boiled custard for us as a sauce for fruit. It serves well as a soft filling between cake layers, or in a thinner version, as a sauce over fruitcakes.

Heat 2 cups skim or 2% lowfat milk with an inch of vanilla bean. Beat 1 egg with 3 tablespoons sugar and 3 tablespoons cornstarch. Add some of the hot milk to this mixture, blend well, and then return it all to the saucepan. Cook, stirring, until thickened, about 3 minutes. When cool, remove the vanilla bean and stir in ½ teaspoon vanilla extract. Makes about 2¼ cups.

To make Custard Sauce, decrease the sugar to 2 tablespoons and the cornstarch to 2 teaspoons. When boiling, stir in 1 tablespoon light honey. This makes a fairly thin sauce. For a thicker sauce, increase the cornstarch to 1 tablespoon.

# *Appendix*

## *Pan Sizes and Capacities*

Pans are measured by the top inside measurement. Square and rectangular pans, because they are deeper, have greater capacities than the nearly same-sized round pans. Measurements are in inches and the capacities given are approximate. Remember too that a cake batter should never completely fill the pan, as it always expands and rises.

| Round Pans | Capacities | Square pans | |
|---|---|---|---|
| 8 x 1½ layer pan | 4 cups | 7 x 7 x 1½ pan | 4 cups |
| 9 x 1½ layer pan | 5 cups | 8 x 8 x 2 pan | 6 cups |
| 8 x 2½ springform | 5 cups | 9 x 9 x 2 pan | 8 cups |
| 9 x 2½ springform | 6 cups | **Rectangular pans** | |
| 7½ x 3 bundt pan | 6 cups | 7 x 10¾ x 1½ | 6 cups |
| 9 x 4 bundt pan | 9 cups | 9 x 13 x 2 | 12 cups |
| 9 x 4½ tube pan | 12 cups | 10 x 14 x 2 | 16 cups |
| 10 x 4½ tube pan | 18 cups | **Loaf pans** | |
| | | 3⅝ x 7⅜ x 2¼ | 3 cups |
| | | 5 x 9 x 3 | 6 cups |

# Substitutions and Equivalents

When baking cakes, one can often substitute ingredients in a traditional recipe which will boost protein, fiber, vitamin and mineral content and/or cut down on the total fat, the saturated fat, calories, sugar, and sodium. For a few general rules: you can substitute about ½ cup honey for 1 cup of sugar. You may wish to decrease the other liquid in the recipe somewhat. If you use less salt than the traditional recipe calls for, you will need less sweetening (a double benefit) as your cake will taste sweeter.

| *Instead of* | *Try* |
| --- | --- |
| Butter, margarine, shortening | Monounsaturated and polyunsaturated oil; use less |
| Whole milk | Skim milk, 2% milk; nonfat dry milk diluted half and half with water |
| Sour cream | Sour skim milk, buttermilk, plain lowfat yogurt |
| Cream cheese | Part skim or lite ricotta, lowfat cream cheese, lowfat cottage cheese, farmer cheese |
| 1 whole egg | 2 egg whites (for up to 2 eggs) |
| Cake flour | 1 cup all-purpose flour less 2 tablespoons |
| White flour | Whole wheat pastry flour, oat flour, soy flour (small quantity), wheat germ |
| White sugar | Honey (use ½ the amount), undiluted fruit juice concentrates (adjust liquid) |
| Brown sugar | Dark honey, molasses (use ½ the amount), undiluted fruit juice concentrate |

## Useful Substitutions

| | |
|---|---|
| 1 teaspoon baking powder | ½ teaspoon cream of tartar plus ¼ teaspoon baking soda |
| 1 tablespoon cornstarch | 2 tablespoons flour or potato starch |
| 1 cup milk | ½ cup evaporated milk plus ½ cup water or |
| | ⅓ cup dry milk plus liquid to make 1 cup |
| 1 cup sour milk, buttermilk | 1 tablespoon lemon juice plus sweet milk to make 1 cup |
| 1 ounce unsweetened chocolate | 3 tablespoons cocoa plus 1 tablespoon margarine |

# Index